A VISITOR'S GUIDE TO

LONDON'S
ROYAL PARKS

To Lesley Palumbo, who gave me my dream job of managing parks in Watford, Hertfordshire, for over 11 years.

A VISITOR'S GUIDE TO
LONDON'S ROYAL PARKS

PAUL RABBITTS

WHITE OWL

AN IMPRINT OF PEN & SWORD BOOKS LTD.
YORKSHIRE – PHILADELPHIA

First published in Great Britain in 2025 by
White Owl
An imprint of
Pen & Sword Books Ltd.
Yorkshire - Philadelphia

ISBN 978 1 03611 487 9

Design: SJmagic DESIGN SERVICES, India.

The Publisher's authorised representative in the EU for product
safety is Authorised Rep Compliance Ltd., Ground Floor, 71
Lower Baggot Street, Dublin D02 P593, Ireland.
www.arccompliance.com

For a complete list of Pen & Sword titles please contact

PEN & SWORD BOOKS LIMITED
George House, Beevor Street, Off Pontefract Road, Hoyle Mill,
Barnsley, South Yorkshire, England, S71 1HN.
E-mail: enquiries@pen-and-sword.co.uk
Website: www.pen-and-sword.co.uk

or

PEN AND SWORD BOOKS
1950 Lawrence Rd, Havertown, PA 19083, USA
E-mail: uspen-and-sword@casematepublishers.com
Website: www.penandswordbooks.com

MIX
Paper | Supporting
responsible forestry
FSC™ C016779

CONTENTS

INTRODUCTION

A quick search of any good online book retailer or a browse of the shelves of any independent London bookseller for 'London's Royal Parks' will bring up a plethora of books that have been written over many years, from Jacob Larwood's *The Story of the London Parks* in 1900, to more recently, a few written by myself on Hyde Park, Regent's Park and Richmond Park. Yet what you won't find is an up-to-date guide for the many visitors to these majestic open spaces. There are nearly 80 million visits to the Royal Parks every year, making them the most popular destinations in the capital. In 1956, author, poet and critic, Richard Thomas Church (1893–1972) wrote *The Royal Parks of London*, which was published by The Ministry of Public Buildings and Works as a guide book at a cost of 3s 6d net. It was republished in 1965, 1967 and once again in 1993 with 'amendments'. This was followed up by *London's Royal Parks Souvenir Guide* published by the Royal Parks organisation in 1993. Thirty years have passed and the parks continue to thrive, with new additions, events and celebrations. However, any visitor today will be overwhelmed by the beauty of these historic spaces that boast royal palaces, boathouses, bandstands, lodges, gatehouses, ornamental gardens, sculpture, public art, memorials and places for repose and refreshments. Today the Royal Parks as a charitable organisation is responsible for the care and maintenance of a large collection of historical built assets, comprised primarily of monuments, structures and buildings within the parks, and associated boundaries, with 166 of them listed by Historic England, including the Grade I Albert Memorial in Kensington Gardens.

What is apparent from the time of Richard Church's description of these parks and his later versions are the many changes that have occurred throughout their history, with new introductions, many controversial, including memorials to monarchs, tragedies and celebratory events. London is a city in constant flux. Church in his opening introduction acknowledges such changes citing: 'London, formerly so much abused as the epitome of urban dirt and darkness, the scene of most of Dickens's more dismal nightmares, has gradually changed her appearance, especially during the past twenty-five years. She may be a most venerable lady, two thousand years old, but lately she has had a face-lift, and some of her own children hardly know her... she has been fortunate in possessing, at her very centre, a group of open spaces.'

The importance of these Royal Parks is further emphasised as he describes how a 'visitor would come up from the Kentish countryside on a summer day, walk out of Charing Cross Station, under the Admiralty Arch, and follow the parks westward almost as far as Shepherd's Bush, his route along the Mall, round by Buckingham Palace, along Constitution Hill, across Hyde Park Corner into the Park, along the Serpentine to Kensington Gardens, over Holland Walk or through the recently opened Holland Park – not itself a Royal Park – out to the Avenue that leads westward. He might even foster the illusion that he had never landed in London, and that he was taking an uninterrupted rural ride.' It is a little

different today, and I would certainly avoid the Mall, preferring to walk through St James's Park from Horse Guards Parade.

I sincerely hope this book serves as an up to date guide to this 'group of open spaces'. What the book is not, though, is a detailed guide with proposed routes to follow. The intention is for the user to gain a greater understanding of how these parks came about, but also to widen the visitor's knowledge of some of the more unusual aspects of London's Royal Parks and to simply encourage the visitor to meander at will – the best way to discover the many pleasures within the Royal Parks in my humble opinion. If you want to know what's occurring daily in the Royal Parks, you simply need to go to their website. It is packed with information.

https://www.royalparks.org.uk/

We shall start with the oldest Royal Park – Greenwich Park, the birthplace of the Tudors.

GREENWICH PARK
BIRTHPLACE OF THE TUDORS

'Where burthen'd Thames reflect the crowded sail
Commercial care and busy toil prevail
Whoese murky veil, aspiring to the skies
Obscures thy beauty, and thy form denies
Save where thy spires pierce the doubtful air
As gleams of hope amidst a world of care'
J.M.W. Turner (1775–1851)

Over 100 years later, Richard Church in his 1956 guide introduces the park, writing that 'People who are inclined to associate Greenwich Park with the somewhat dreary approaches from Central London will be surprised when they discover this highly individual place, a beauty-spot in its own right, deserving fame other than that which it has possessed as the determinant of the degrees of longitude.' It is indeed a surprise and the park would count itself as one of the most beautiful spots in London, with one of the finest views in the metropolis. Likewise, the Honourable Mrs Evelyn Cecil wrote in 1907: '... it would not occur to most people to reckon Greenwich among the London Parks. But it is well within the bounds of the County of London, and now so easy of access that it should have no difficulty in substantiating its claim to be one of the most beautiful among them. Both for natural features and historic interest it is one of the most fascinating.' Turner, Church and Cecil are all unequivocal in their admiration of the 'beauty' of this place.

Historically, Greenwich Park is the oldest of the Royal Parks. Since Roman times there has been a settlement of some kind on the site of Greenwich Park. This prominence was known to be the site of an important residence before it was inherited by Henry V's brother Humphrey, Duke of Gloucester,

The encroaching skyline of modern London overlooking this ancient landscape. © Allan Harris

in 1427. On 30 January 1433, the King's Council of England granted to Duke Humphrey and his Duchess, Eleanor, a licence to 'empark 200 acres of land, pasture, weed, heath and furze at Estgrenewich.' The duke and duchess were also given permission to enclose their manor house and manor of Estgrenewich with a wall 'to crenelate the same and to build a tower of stone

and mortar in the park'. Greenwich therefore became the first Royal Park to be enclosed.

Duke Humphrey was uncle and protector of the young king, Henry VI.

He was also a learned scholar and is remembered less for his founding of Greenwich Park than for the collection of manuscripts he left to Oxford University, which eventually formed the basis of the famous Bodleian Library. The duke was an ambitious man who married an equally ambitious woman who wished to see her husband king of England instead of being just the king's uncle and advisor. Unfortunately for her, she was suspected of being a witch and the king eventually committed her to prison for high treason for the remainder of her life when he heard of her desires. Not long after, in 1447, Duke Humphrey was arrested and several days later died in mysterious circumstances in prison.

Almost immediately, Greenwich was seized by Margaret of Anjou, the young queen of Henry VI. She took up residence in the house which she called 'Plesaunce'. At this time and for many years after, the keeper or ranger of the park also looked after the palace, or 'Manor of Plesaunce' or 'Placentia' as it was also known, the tower, the great and little gardens and the orchard nearby – all for the amount of 1s. 4d. a day. Almost 100 years later Henry VII practically rebuilt Duke Humphrey's manor house at the cost of some £3,000 and spent that amount again on decorating what became his favourite palace.

Greenwich became the birthplace of Henry VIII and for much of his life he spent time in the palace or partaking of sport in the park. There were regular jousts and tournaments as well as Christmas games, and he came every year to 'bring in the

May'. It was also the birthplace of his two daughters who became Mary I, daughter of Catherine of Aragon, his first queen, and Elizabeth I, daughter of Anne Boleyn, his second queen. Edward VI, only son of Henry VIII, by his third wife Jane Seymour, died at Greenwich Palace in 1553 before he was 16 years old. Henry's fourth wife, Anne of Cleves, was escorted to Greenwich to meet him for the first time before their marriage at the palace in 1540. It was here at Greenwich for much of the first half of his reign, that Henry spent most of his time, and it was to become the diplomatic and political centre of the country. On 2 July 1559, the year after her accession, the City of London entertained Elizabeth I in Greenwich Park. Richly dressed in 'coats of velvet and chaines of gold, with guns, moris pikes, halberds and flags', 1,400 men-at-arms marched from London to give a military display in her presence. She shared her father's love of Greenwich Palace and it was to become one of her favourite homes, spending much of her time between her regular 'progresses' around the kingdom, returning via the Thames in the gilded royal barge.

When James I came to the throne, he replaced the wooden fence round the park with a brick wall, 3.5 metres high and 2 miles long, some of which still remains in the park to this day. He gifted the palace and park to his Danish wife, Queen Anne, who commissioned the court architect, Inigo Jones, to design a special home for her in the park. This building, in Palladian style, was known as the 'House of Delights' or the Queen's House. When Anne died in 1619, James lost interest in the project and presented Greenwich to the Prince of Wales, later to become Charles I. When Charles became king in 1625, Inigo Jones was ordered to complete the Queen's House for his young French wife, Henrietta Maria.

During the Commonwealth, after the execution of Charles I in 1649, parliament elected to sell the greater part of the royal estate at Greenwich, including the park. However, the sale was nullified in 1656 when it was decided to reserve the park and the Queen's House for the protector, Oliver Cromwell, although he never lived there. When the monarchy was restored in 1660, Charles II had what remained of the crumbling palace demolished and the foundations buried.

In the early 1660s the park was laid out in the French style and many trees were planted. The coppices in the East and West Wilderness – the current deer park and Ranger's Field – were laid out by Sir William Boreman, keeper of the palace and park. The sweet chestnut avenues were planted a year or two later – some still survive. A formal terrace constructed at the north end of the Blackheath Avenue was planted with six hundred elms that enclosed a large rectangular lawn. These trees and terracing were part of the formal scheme that the park retains to this day, a style inspired by the gardens of André le Nôtre, gardener to Louis XIV of France. Much of this original design is part of a major restoration planned and being delivered by the Royal Parks in 2024 as part of the 'Greenwich Revealed' project. Boreman also recorded the planting of 'birch trees, quicksets, ivy berries, holly berries, privie and ashen keys.'

In 1664, Charles II commissioned John Webb, a pupil of Inigo Jones, to build a new palace on the site of the previous one, but only one wing was partly completed due to a lack of funds. King Charles was greatly interested in science and encouraged scientific research by founding in 1662 the Royal Society. In 1675 he commissioned Sir Christopher Wren to build the Royal Observatory on the site of Duke Humphrey's medieval tower. It was named Flamsteed House in about 1720, after John Flamsteed, the first astronomer royal. Now part of the National Maritime Museum, the observatory still contains a comprehensive collection of astronomical instruments and, more importantly, the meridian line, which runs across the courtyard.

When James II married his second wife, Mary of Modena, he presented her with Greenwich Park and the

Prospect of Greenwich from the Observatory at the Top of the Hill, 1752. © Yale Center for British Art, Paul Mellon Collection

Queen's House. It was from Greenwich that she sailed for France in 1688 with her little son into exile at the end of her husband's brief three-year reign. Royal interest in Greenwich declined during the reigns of Mary II and William III and they rarely visited the park. Queen Mary donated the unfinished Charles II building and the rest of the palace site for a hospital for seamen. Sir Christopher Wren completed the overall design free of charge, but the Royal Naval Hospital, as it became known as, was not finished for over a century.

Gradual public access was granted at about the time Queen Anne came to the throne in 1702, first to pensioners, and, in a somewhat limited way, to the general public. From early in the eighteenth century until they were suppressed in 1857 the Greenwich Fairs were held in May and October, when much merry-making went on in the park. Queen Anne's desire to preserve the beauty of the park was fostered by her royal gardener, Henry Wise, and her consort, Prince George of Denmark, whom she appointed as ranger. However, there was little evidence in the eighteenth century of any serious interest being taken in the trees, and many decayed or were felled. It was at Greenwich that George I, first of the Hanoverian kings, landed to take possession of his kingdom on 18 September 1714. The following day he held his first reception in the Queen's

House and on 20 September made his entry into London.

Caroline of Anspach as the Princess of Wales, later to become Queen Caroline, wife of George II, extended her enthusiasm for gardening to Greenwich Park where she was ranger from 1730–37. In 1806, during the rangership of Caroline of Brunswick, wife of the Prince Regent (later George IV), the Queen's House was turned into a 'naval asylum' for the children of seamen. Montague House nearby, which Caroline, as Princess of Wales, already occupied, was used as the ranger's residence until about 1815, when it was demolished. Chesterfield House on the park perimeter was purchased and eventually renamed Ranger's House. Another member of the royal family, the Duke of Clarence (later William IV), and brother to George IV, was the next ranger followed by Princess Sophia, daughter of the Duke of Gloucester, in 1816. She kept the rangership until her death in 1844, aged 71 years old. She had lived much of her life at the Ranger's House and was well loved by local people.

Free access to the park seems to have been given to the public during the reign of George IV. In the years that followed, less and less interest was taken in Greenwich Park by the ruling sovereign. By the 1870s the Royal Naval Hospital had no inmates. However the park's naval associations continued and, in 1873, the buildings became the Royal Naval College. In 1825 the Naval Asylum was merged with the Royal Hospital School. The additional buildings which had been erected around the Queen's House soon after the founding of the asylum, in 1806, were also taken over by the school. These buildings continued to house the Royal Hospital School until 1933 when, considerably restored, they became the present National Maritime Museum.

During the Second World War there were anti-aircraft guns in the Flower Garden, and the tips of some of the trees were cut off to widen the field of fire. Evidence of this can still be seen in the truncated shape of some of the trees in the garden. After the war Greenwich Park was restored to its former glory with further improvements made.

The ongoing twentieth century saw three main themes in Greenwich Park; the gradual improvement of facilities and the addition of amenities; the park gradually becoming recognised as an 'historic' park with the Royal Parks management becoming involved with the restoration and conservation of the park's historic character. The century also saw conflict between the pressure of public use and access versus the quality of the environment. In the early twentieth century more lavatories were built, and games pitches and tennis courts were provided as well as a new refreshment kiosk. The playground and boating pond were made. Gates were repaired or replaced and parts of the park wall rebuilt. Against this background of rising tourism and historic interest in Greenwich generally (the *Cutty Sark* was opened to visitors in 1957), the Ministry of Public Buildings and Works looked at the park with a view to restoring its 'historic' plan. Decisions were postponed until the publication of the *7th report of the Advisory Committee on Forestry* (1964) which concluded: '...every effort should now be made to restore the plan of the park as nearly as possible to the layout shown in the seventeenth century print... Greenwich Park is still potentially the finest interpretation in England of a layout based on that grand European seventeenth century conception of design that governed also the grouping of the buildings leading to the river.'

The integrity and quality of the park continued to be monitored by local groups. In 1959 the Greenwich Society was formed and successfully opposed a road improvement scheme through Crooms Hill. The society helped to get an area including Greenwich Park and Blackheath designated as the first Conservation Area in London in 1967. A proposed 1968 road across the north of the park was also dropped after local and national opposition. The Friends of Greenwich Park, established in 1992, played a major role in helping to protect the integrity of the park, including supporting several restoration projects. In 1993 the Rose Garden was redesigned with the support of the Friends of Greenwich Park. The whole

park, neighbouring properties and part of Greenwich town centre were inscribed on UNESCO's World Heritage List in 1997. The closure of the Royal Naval College and its conversion to a charitable trust provided a site for the University of Greenwich and Trinity Laban School of Music. The Cutty Sark station opened in 1999 as part of the Docklands Light Railway extension southward and since it was opened Greenwich has become a significant hub due to the link with the Isle of Dogs financial centre. In 2011 the borough gifted the land of the Queen's Orchard to the Royal Parks. In 2012 Greenwich Park hosted the equestrian, modern pentathlon and paralympic equestrian events for the London Olympic games.

To this day the park is still given a strong identity by the resilience of the 'Grand Plan' design of the seventeenth century. The striking element of Greenwich is the fusion between the dramatic natural topography of the site and the formal artificial layout of its avenues. Its status as a Royal Park, as well as its integral relationship with the buildings within and adjoining the site, gives the historic layout of Greenwich Park special significance, as identified in its World Heritage Site status.

In 1995, the *Royal Parks Review* described Greenwich as unique: 'a place of pilgrimage, as increasing numbers of visitors obviously demonstrate, a place for inspiration, imagination and sheer pleasure. Majestic buildings, park, views, unseen meridian and a wealth of history form a unified whole of international importance. The maintenance and management of this great place requires sensitivity and constant care.'

Returning to Richard Church's guide of 1956, he concludes his description of Greenwich Park, describing it as 'a peaceful retreat... but it still overlooks the centre of the British Commonwealth, at Meridian Zero, and holds its awe-inspiring place between the Eastern and Western hemispheres.'

NOT TO BE MISSED ON A VISIT TO GREENWICH PARK

The Queen's House

Greenwich Park has much to offer and its status as to why it is a UNESCO World Heritage Site is clear when you visit. The buildings within and its wider setting are simply breath-taking. Of all the buildings and attractions, one of the finest is the Queen's House, England's first classical building built by self-styled architect Inigo Jones, who was commissioned by Anne of Denmark in 1616 to build this unique house. The Queen's House is exceptional in both style and characteristics in comparison to other English buildings of the time. Jones created a first-floor central bridge that joined the two halves of the building. He was considerably inspired by Italian Renaissance architecture and the Palladian style, created by Andrea Palladio. What Jones did was to apply the characteristics of harmony, detail, and proportion to this commission. Rather than being in the traditional, red-brick Tudor style like the then existing palace, the house is white and is known for its elegant proportions. Jones felt compelled to reflect political circumstances of the time through his use of his Orders, reflected in his 'Roman Sketchbook' notes.

Inigo Jones' design is also famous for two of its aspects: the Great Hall and the Tulip staircase. The Great Hall is the centrepiece of the Queen's House and holds a first-floor gallery that overlooks geometric-styled black and white marble flooring. The Great Hall is recognisable and innovative for its architecture. Much like Jones' inspiration for the rest of the Queen's House, Jones used the rules of proportion created by Palladio. The Tulip staircase was an unusual feature during this period and the first of its kind. Made of ornate wrought iron, it is Britain's first geometric and unsupported staircase. Each tread is cantilevered from the wall and supported by the step below, a design invented by the mason, Nicholas Stone. Each step is interlocked along the bottom of the riser. Jones found inspiration for the staircase, and the glass lantern above, from Palladio's

The Queen's House. © Peter Jeffree

Carita Monastery, where he noted that the staircases with a void in the centre 'succeed very well because they can have light from above'. Jones hired Nicholas Stone to lay the black and white flooring which mirrored the design of the ceiling.

The Old Royal Observatory

Overlooking the Queen's House is the former Royal Observatory which is now based at Cambridge. The Old Royal Observatory here in Greenwich Park is now a museum and is a magnet for tourists all year round. In 1675 Sir Christopher Wren was asked to work on the Royal Observatory at Greenwich, the first purpose-built scientific research facility in the country and a commission close to his heart. Wren and Robert Hooke clearly had an intense interest in all aspects of science, including geometry, optics and in astronomy. Hooke was almost certainly involved in much of the design of the Royal Observatory, built at the top of the hill on the foundations of a tower which had been part of the old Greenwich Castle. As a result, it was aligned thirteen degrees away from true north, much to the annoyance of the astronomer royal, John Flamsteed, a difficult man to deal with at the best

Flamsteed House and the Old Royal Observatory. © Raymond Cunningham

of times. In the adjacent garden is Flamsteed's Well. It was here that the astronomer used to lie on a mattress at the bottom of its 100-foot drop to make observations through a glass.

Known as Flamsteed House, with its red brick turrets, it was hoped that this would solve the 'longitude problem' that bedevilled early navigation. The red time ball on the eastern turret was installed in 1833 and is dropped daily at 1pm as a signal to boats on the Thames.

The Royal Naval Hospital

Looking back from the Royal Observatory, one of the finest views in London opens up with its ever changing horizon and skyline evolving with modern skyscrapers, centres of finance and commerce dominating. Yet in the foreground are a number of buildings that once dominated this scene.

It was a few months before Queen Mary's death, when the work had been stopped at Hampton Court, that led to one of Wren's finest buildings here at Greenwich. In 1694, the Royal Hospital for Seamen was founded as a residential home for injured sailors on the instructions of Queen Mary II. She had become foundress of a building project but with a very different purpose. This was to be the Royal Naval Hospital at Greenwich,

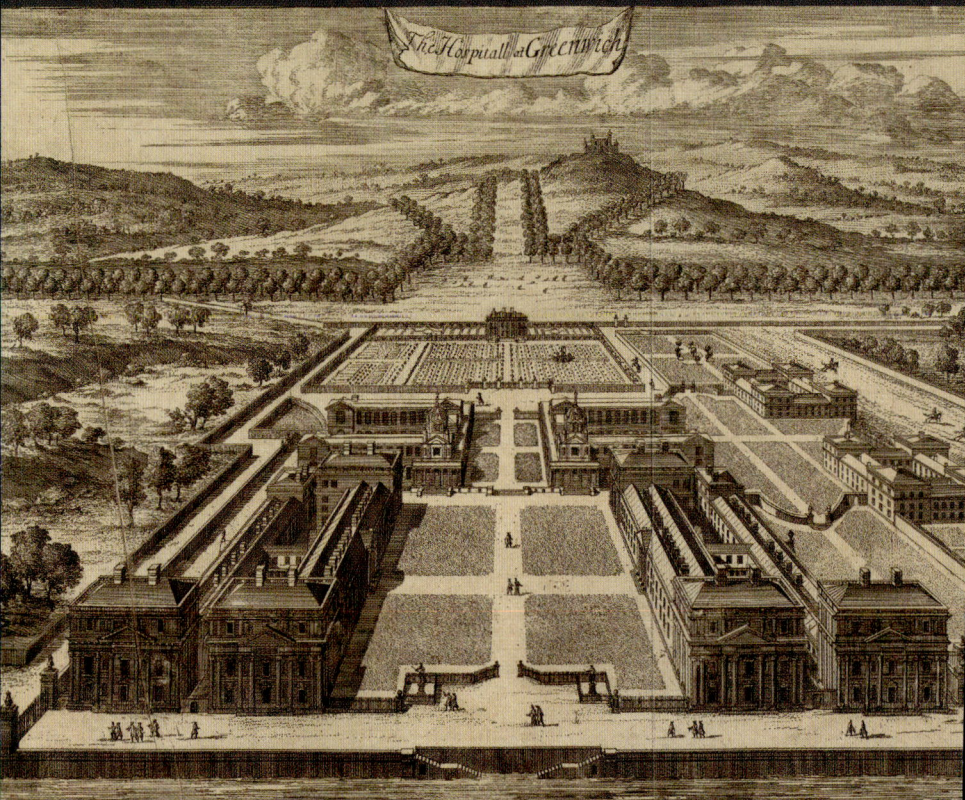

The Hospital at Greenwich, 1755. © Yale Center for British Art, Paul Mellon Collection

for which she and William granted the site of Greenwich Palace. It was to be the naval counterpart of Chelsea, and it seems to have been due to Queen Mary's 'fixt intention for Magnificence' that it should outstrip Chelsea in architectural splendour. It was one of the last undertakings in which Wren was personally concerned as chief designer. Greenwich had been a royal palace, and as such Charles II had fully intended to rebuild it. One block of the new palace had in fact been finished soon after the restoration. The decision was made in 1694 with the existing palace block to be adapted for its new purpose with a new block by Wren built alongside it. Wren proceeded to devise a symmetrical layout for the whole hospital. Little remains of the original layout of 1695, but Wren's personal work at Greenwich extends to the Painted Hall and the twin domes.

The Old Royal Naval Hospital.

Architect Nicholas Hawksmoor was certainly involved and was likely to have been responsible for much of the detailing and work on the domes too. The hall was structurally complete by 1702, the year in which Queen Anne came to the throne and when Wren reached the age of seventy.

National Maritime Museum

This great panorama of Greenwich is one of the finest views in London and also unfolds along the path that lies in front of the National Maritime Museum. The wings were completed in 1809 and are linked to Inigo Jones' Queen's House by colonnades built to commemorate the Battle of Trafalgar. The Queen's House formed a striking contrast with the rambling red brick Tudor palace on the waterfront. When the house was built, the Deptford to Woolwich road ran between the palace gardens and the park. This posed a problem, which the architect, Christopher Wren, ingeniously solved by designing the house in two blocks connected by a bridge that spanned the road.

In front of the Queen's House, looking up towards Flamsteed House, is a vast

Greenwich, with London in the distance, c.1680.
© Yale Center for British Art, Paul Mellon Collection

The Queen's House in the foreground, the National Maritime Museum with connecting colonnades. © Peter Jeffree

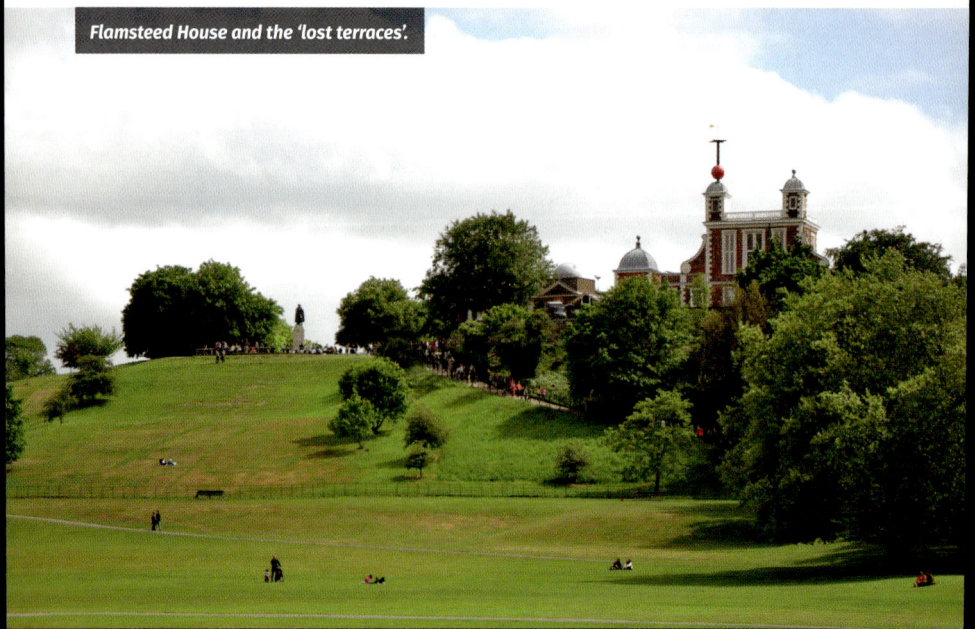

Flamsteed House and the 'lost terraces'.

expanse of lawn and is all that remains of the terrace that was to form the centrepiece of Charles II's landscaping, often attributed to Le Nôtre and gradually being restored to its past glory.

The Ranger's House

Another building to seek out whilst in Greenwich Park is of course the Ranger's House, a fine eighteenth century house on the western edge of the park. It was built in 1699. From 1748–1772 the Ranger's House was the home of Lord Chesterfield, a notable statesman, writer and gardener and was renamed Chesterfield House. When the neighbouring Montague House, former home of ranger Princess Caroline of Brunswick (1768–1821), estranged wife of George IV, was demolished in 1816, Chesterfield House became the residence for the holders of the royal office of the ranger of Greenwich Park. The last ranger, Viscount Wolseley (1833–1913), departed in 1896, leaving the house empty. Its 15 acre garden, created for Montague House by Princess Caroline, had already been returned to the park. Whilst the princess was ranger, her tenure was most notable because of her private life, which led to a 'delicate investigation' into her behaviour. Since 1986 the Ranger's House has been in

A View of the Ranger's House in the Park and of the Town of Greenwich. © Yale Center for British Art, Paul Mellon Collection

The Ranger's House. © Peter Jeffree

the care of Historic England and is now home to the Wernher collection which focuses on early renaissance Italian art and decorative arts.

Major General James Wolfe

Many of the Royal Parks are rich in sculpture, statues and memorials. Greenwich Park is virtually devoid of such features, yet has one which dominates as you climb the hill towards the old observatory. Overlooking the park stands the statue of Major General James Wolfe (1727–59). Born in Westerham, Kent, he was the eldest son of General Edward Wolfe. William Pitt the Elder, Earl of Chatham, gave Wolfe command of 9,000 men to sail up the St Lawrence and try to dislodge the French from Quebec. He defeated them by getting his men to climb the cliffs in the dark and take the French by surprise.

The statue of General Wolfe. © Peter Jeffree

In the ensuing Battle of the Plains of Abraham, Wolfe was fatally wounded, but this great victory meant the end of French rule in North America. Wolfe lived for a time at Macartney House in Greenwich, and is buried in nearby St Alfege church. The statue is the work of the Canadian sculptor Robert Tait McKenzie, and was a gift from the Canadian people. It was unveiled in 1930 by the Marquis de Montcalm, who was descended from the French general defeated by Wolfe at Quebec.

Queen Caroline's poor hygiene

One of the more unusual features of the park are the remains of a bath belonging to Queen Caroline which are found close to Chesterfield Gate in the south-west corner of Greenwich Park. She held notoriously boisterous parties and, in the early years of the nineteenth century, there were rumours circulating that she had an illegitimate child. Investigated by a royal commission, she was cleared of adultery but they reported that her behaviour was open to 'unfavourable interpretations'. She left England for Europe in 1814 and Montague House was demolished a year later leaving only the outline of her bath, which can still be seen against the wall to the left of the Ranger's House. Her lack of personal hygiene was well known, noticeable even on her wedding night. The bath itself was filled in during the 1980s and for nearly 20 years the only sign of it was a plaque which stated 'A bath beneath the paving and this wall are all that remains of Montague House, the house between 1801 and 1813 of the Princess of Wales, later to become Queen Caroline, wife of George IV.' In 2001, the Royal Parks excavated the bath with funding from the Friends of Greenwich Park, Greenwich Society, the Friends of Ranger's House and individual donations.

The remains of Queen Caroline's bath. © Mike Grice

A Hidden Gem at Greenwich Park – One Tree Hill

One Tree Hill is found in the north-west corner of the park and is a narrow, north-west facing spur from the main Blackheath plateau and from old images, was well known for 'tumbling'. The Conduit Head on the lower face of One Tree Hill is a Grade II listed structure, part of an important and historically influential system of water gathering grounds within the geological layers, having been of considerable significance in the siting and development of the earlier Tudor palace. It was one of the three known conduit heads or houses which served

The view from One Tree Hill today. © John Tiffin

One Tree Hill, Greenwich, with London in the Distance, 1779. © Yale Center for British Art, Paul Mellon Collection

Queen Elizabeth's oak – c.800 years old and fell down in 1991. The hollow interior was once paved and used as a 'prison' for offenders against the park rules. © Harvey Edser

the Royal Hospital for Seamen. Queen Elizabeth's Oak is an ancient oak which fell in 1991. Henry VIII is supposed to have danced with Anne Boleyn under the tree. Other stories tell of Queen Elizabeth taking tea inside the hollow trunk and that this space was later used to incarcerate those who contravened the park's regulations. Historic England have dated the tree to 1292.

INVOLVED WITH GREENWICH PARK

Sir Christopher Wren (1632–1723)

Sir Christopher Wren is famously known and recognised as the architect of St. Paul's Cathedral but his first loves were science and mathematics. During the early part of his career he worked as an astronomer. The Royal Observatory here at Greenwich combines both aspects of his work: astronomy and architecture. In 1657, when Wren was only 25 years old, he was appointed Professor of Astronomy at Gresham College, London. It was here that a group of scientists met regularly to discuss their ideas. This group formed the core of what would later become the Royal Society. After several more years spent on scientific research, Wren became Savilian Professor of Astronomy at Oxford in 1661. Wren's work still surrounds us today, and includes both churches and secular buildings, particularly in the City of London. Some of his other most well-known buildings include the South Front of Hampton Court Palace, Kensington Palace, the Monument to the Great Fire of London and Marlborough House.

Wren's interest in architecture developed from his study of physics and engineering. At a time when architecture was considered to be a part-time interest for wealthy and educated gentlemen, Wren was one of the few architects to have a sound knowledge of the structure of buildings. In 1675, Wren received the commission here in Greenwich from Charles II, it was clear that this must have been of special interest to him. The king hoped that a proper study of the moon and the stars would help to perfect navigation at sea. Using telescopes and other instruments in the new observatory, the astronomers would record the moon's position relative to certain stars at set times. This would enable navigators to fix their position at sea more accurately. The night sky would, in effect, become the sailor's clock. It was hoped in this way to avoid the growing loss of life and ships' cargoes in shipwrecks.

To save money, second-hand building materials were used to build the observatory. Brick and stone were brought along the River Thames from an old Tudor fort at Tilbury that was being repaired. Other money came from the sale of old gunpowder. In spite of these limitations, Wren managed to create the beautiful Octagon Room. Underneath the Octagon Room, the observatory included the living quarters for the Royal Astronomer.

In 1682, Wren designed a royal hospital for soldiers at Chelsea. The idea of building a similar hospital at Greenwich for injured and disabled seamen may have been that of King James II. As Admiral of the Fleet, he

Christopher Wren by Godfrey Kneller 1711.

had seen much action at sea. However, nothing was done during his short reign, and it was left to Queen Mary to put the plan into action. Wren's original scheme was to build a three-sided arrangement of buildings, incorporating a block by James Webb which had originally been intended as a new palace for King Charles II. Queen Mary insisted that the view of the Queen's House from the river should be kept, so Wren adapted his plan. The hospital was finished in 1702, in the reign of Queen Anne.

Wren died in 1723 at the age of 91. His achievements during his long life were considerable, including the introduction of the Baroque style to Britain, though he gave it a more restrained flavour than on the continent. He was also one of the first professional architects in this country to have a sound knowledge of engineering.

André Le Nôtre (1613–1700)

The French landscape architect André Le Nôtre, or Le Nostre, gave to the art of the formal garden its most monumental and definitive expression. His style spread to every corner of Europe as can be seen here at Greenwich, even though he never visited.

Born in Paris, Le Nôtre was educated very early in his career in the practical aspects of gardening procedure, being both the son and grandson of gardeners who had worked at the Palace of the Tuileries. Though Le Nôtre succeeded to the position of his father as chief gardener at the Tuileries in 1637, it was not until he began his work on Nicolas Fouquet's château of Vaux-le-Vicomte in 1655 that the landscape architect became famous. Here, in collaboration with the architect Louis Le Vau, Le Nôtre had for the first time the opportunity to create an entire château and garden complex. Throughout, there is a spirit of ordered discipline, geometric formality, and perfect equilibrium among the various components – fountains, sculptures, parterres, and architectural elements.

Upon the completion of Vaux in 1661, Le Nôtre was active in the service of King Louis XIV, redesigning the gardens of Fontainebleau, Saint-Germain-en-Laye, and the Tuileries. Le Nôtre's masterpiece was the vast garden project for Versailles, which he began in 1662 and which engaged his talents throughout the remainder of the century. For Louis XIV he also executed the gardens of the Grand Trianon and Clagny, and for the French nobility he designed the splendid garden complexes of Sceaux, Chantilly, Meudon, Saint-Cloud and Pontchartrain. In referring to Le Nôtre's death on 15 September 1700, the *Mercure de France* wrote, 'The king has just lost a man rare and zealous for his service, a man who, very singular in his art, did him great honor.'

André Le Nôtre, remembered outside the palm house in Sefton Park, Liverpool.

ANDRE LE NOTRE
The most Famous of Gardener Architects
Born at Paris 1613   Died at Paris 1700

Inigo Jones (1573–1652)

Inigo Jones was a notable British painter, architect, and designer who founded the English classical tradition of architecture. He was born in Smithfield, London at the home of a cloth worker. Little is known about the architect's early life but it is said that he worked as an internee with a carpenter and travelled across the whole continent between 1596 to 1605 and learned advanced architectural skills. Later, between 1613–1614, Jones made his trip to Italy and stayed there for a while to learn professional studies of Palladio's architecture and architectural theories. Inigo Jones' professional career started off in 1603 by serving at the court of King Christian IV of Denmark and Norway, and later in 1615 he got the appointment by James I at the court as the surveyor of the king's works and chief architect. He secured this position until 1642 when the outbreak of war and subsequent disruption of court life brought his stay there to an end.

Jones is regarded as the very first English architect with core professionalism and he is held responsible for turning English architecture from its essentially medieval Gothic and Tudor traditions into the conventional Italian Renaissance manner. The project that gained him immense recognition was the Queen's House here at Greenwich that was also one of his first projects carried out in 1616. Many of Jones' buildings didn't survive but fortunately this Queen's House is one that did.

Jones became the most desired architect of the 1630s but his services were provided to only a limited circle of notable and prominent people of those times. There are hundreds of buildings associated with Jones' name but architectural historians authenticate a very small number of them to be on his credit. What his impact was though was his significant influence and inspiration on a large number of architects of the eighteenth century, and many structures including bridges and roads have been named after him.

Portrait of Inigo Jones, English Architect (c. 1757–1758).

John Flamsteed (1646–1719)

John Flamsteed was the first astronomer royal and director of the Royal Observatory at Greenwich from 1675. He was appointed as King Charles II's 'astronomical observator' on 4 March 1675. In effect, even though he was the first astronomer royal, the title was not yet formally attached to his post. His task was to run the new Royal Observatory shortly to be built at Greenwich, and he remained in charge there until his death on the last day of 1719. His *Historia Coelestis Britannica* (1725), containing a new star catalogue of unprecedented accuracy, and *Atlas Coelestis* (1729), containing celestial charts, were posthumous publications completed by his widow Margaret and assistants. An earlier *Historia Coelestis* (1712) was edited for a committee by Edmond Halley without Flamsteed's cooperation or approval. Most copies were later destroyed by Flamsteed, but

Sundial and Rose Garden in the Grounds of Herstmonceux Castle, East Sussex, with bust of John Flamsteed, first astronomer royal and founder of Greenwich Observatory. © Gerry Morris

it was nevertheless important as the first publication to contain an English star catalogue.

His early life began when he attended a Derby grammar school but sadly he was not allowed to go on to university because of his ill health (a rheumatic complaint) and his father's need for help with business. While he remained at home his father taught him arithmetic, and he was encouraged to further studies by friends interested in practical mathematics, astronomy, and astrology. In November 1669 he addressed a long letter containing astronomical predictions to the Royal Society, which secured his introduction to London scientific circles. In the following year he visited London, passing through Cambridge along the way and obtaining nominal admission to Jesus College. This seems to have been arranged for him by a Fellow of the College, Richard Wroe, who was named as his tutor. Four years later, Flamsteed returned briefly to Cambridge and gained his MA degree by royal mandate, which meant he was not required to stay for the usual number of terms.

During his second visit to Jesus College, Flamsteed wrote a letter to his patron Sir Jonas Moore. Dated 30 June 1674 it assures Moore that he is continuing his previous studies in astronomy. A long discussion of solar tables is followed by comments on more general astronomical topics, including a query about Robert Hooke's claim to have found a method of observing stars during the daytime.

3

BUSHY PARK
A ROYAL SLEEPING BEAUTY

'Bushy has more of the nature of a home farm, and 'indeed' in parts of it one might be deceived into thinking that London was two hundred miles away, beyond the high hedgerows, the tiny streams and foot-bridges, the meadow gates and the sound of the farm machinery at work,' as Richard Church wrote of this least known of the Royal Parks in 1956. Since then of course, London has grown considerably and continues to pry through the entrances of Bushy Park, but never quite dares to enter.

Bushy Park lies within a loop of the River Thames and has been settled

Bushy Park and a timeless landscape. © Peter Jeffree

for at least 4,000 years. Bronze Age barrows have been excavated here with findings such as a fine dagger near to Sandy Lane. Roe deer, boar and beaver would have thrived here within the dense woodland and there is also evidence of early farming in the north-east area, just outside the park boundary. Medieval pot shards have been found and there are clear examples of medieval field boundaries as well as ridge and furrow ploughing. The finest example is found south of the Waterhouse Woodland Gardens where there are traces of the largest and most complete medieval field system in Middlesex.

Long before it became a park, the area to the west belonged to the village of Hampton and was called Eastfield, thus named as it was cultivated land east of the village. It was Sir Giles d'Aubeny who enclosed 162 hectares in 1491, on the site of what would become the Middle Park. In 1514, work began on Hampton Court Palace for Cardinal Wolsey who also acquired an additional 162 hectares and enclosed it with a fence made of oak paling. In total, Wolsey had three separate parks enclosed from ploughed farmland: Bushy Park, Middle Park and Hare Warren. In addition to this, he also had the Home Park of Hampton Court Palace itself.

Hampton Court Palace was eventually 'gifted' to Henry VIII in 1529 and once it was acquired by the king, he commenced many changes to the palace and parks. The small Home Park and what is now known as Bushy Park formed the king's deer park for the palace, where he replaced much of the oak paling with a brick wall, with sections of this still remaining, in particular from the north-west corner of Hampton Court Green, along the northern side of Hampton Court Road to Hampton Wick. James I made further changes to Bushy Park. In 1620, almost 68 hectares were taken into the park on the Hampton side and also enclosed by a wall, with remnants of this still existing. An avenue of lime trees was planted in 1622 which would become the famous Chestnut Avenue much later in the century.

The ornamental waterworks in Bushy Park and at Hampton Court Palace were initiated by Charles I. The engineering for the time was simply remarkable and was initiated by Nicholas Lane who managed to direct water from the River Colne to Hampton Court and the parks. A canal exceeding 12 miles was dug by hand and each parish made responsible for the section within its boundaries. At a cost of £4,000 (over £700,000 in 2024), it was completed in nine months. This waterway is known as the Longford River, and is a major part of the landscape of Bushy Park today, flowing through meadows and open ground. One branch flows from the Diana

Hampton Court Park. 'Hold hard, Gentlemen!'
© Yale Center for British Art, Paul Mellon Collection

fountain through a culvert underneath the road to the canal in Hampton Court Gardens and the Long Water in Hampton Court Park, before joining the River Thames. Another branch, the Queen's River, tumbles over a waterfall at the entrance to the southern Waterhouse Woodland Gardens to supply the Diana fountain. During the Commonwealth period when Oliver Cromwell took up residence in Hampton Court Palace, this branch was redirected to feed the man-made Heron and the Leg of Mutton Ponds. Each of these engineering feats were all remarkable for their times.

The Diana fountain sits in a prime location in the park today. It was Charles I who had it made, possibly by Fanelli, for his queen, Henrietta Maria. During the time of the Commonwealth, the statue, then called Arethusa, was moved from its original site at Somerset House to the Privy Garden of Hampton Court Palace. In the reign of William III and Mary II, when Sir

Diana, resplendent in the winter sunshine. © Peter Jeffree

Christopher Wren was adding the East Court to Hampton Court Palace, he also designed the setting for the Diana fountain and expanded the plans for Chestnut Avenue. His intention was that this avenue should lead to a new classical northern entrance to Hampton Court Palace, to line up with the Great Hall and form the centrepiece of his design for a projected north façade. The scheme was never completed; the avenue ended at Hampton Court Road and the entrance gate by the Wilderness. Early sketches indicate a large basin of water around the statue, about a quarter of the way from the southern boundary of the park. The road down the centre of Chestnut Avenue was made in 1699 when additional lime avenues and the two inner rows of horse chestnuts (1,767 trees in total) were planted, but it was not until 1713 that the Diana fountain was placed in its present position.

The first Lord Halifax was one of William III's most eminent financiers. In 1709 he bought out the Duke of Grafton, who had been keeper of Bushy Park since 1687, and moved into Lower Lodge, now known as Bushy House. In 1713 he added the keeperships of Middle Park and Hare Warren. At this time the distinction between the three parks broke down and the whole area north of Hampton Court Road eventually became known as Bushy Park. Lord Halifax also constructed the

The Longford River, Bushy Park. © Peter Jeffree

canal in Canal Plantation as part of a much larger scheme extending to the Longford River at Pantile Bridge. When he died, his nephew was created Earl of Halifax and succeeded as ranger.

Timothy Bennet

Halifax's son, the second Earl, is notorious for having created in 1752 what is now known as Cobblers Walk. After the second Earl closed the public right of way through the park, Timothy Bennet, a shoemaker from Hampton Wick, noticed that fewer people were passing his shop from the west on their way to Kingston market, and now had to go the long way round by the road. Timothy Bennet had a principle in life that he was 'unwilling to leave the world worse than he found it' and he resolved to do something about it. The shoemaker said that he was willing to spend £700, a considerable sum in those days, on legal costs to establish a public right of way through the park. After consulting an attorney, he served notice of action on Lord Halifax, who was none too pleased with this impertinence and sent him packing. However, on mature reflection, the earl began to see that there might be something in his claim,

The Timothy Bennet Memorial. © Peter Jeffree

and, fearing the ignominy of public defeat by a shoemaker, he withdrew his opposition and the pathway is enjoyed by the public to this day. Timothy Bennet died two years later when he was 77 years old and was mourned by everyone in his village. The monument was erected in 1900 in his memory.

Lord North, when he was Prime Minister, moved into Bushy House in 1771. As a Member of Parliament he could not accept the rangership, so his wife was created ranger instead. Another celebrated ranger, Prince William, Duke of Clarence (later to become William IV), moved into Bushy House in 1797.

Bushy House. © Peter Jeffree

Since his income was small and he had many children to support, he decided to make Bushy Park pay. At least 768 trees were cut down in his first year as ranger, and much of the land was let to tenant farmers.

From the early years of Queen Victoria's reign, the Chestnut Sunday celebrations were held every spring on the nearest Sunday to 11 May, when the horse chestnuts on Chestnut Avenue were in blossom and at their best. Large crowds would travel to the park on public transport, taking picnics and watching cyclists go by. The celebrations ceased during the Second World War and were not resumed until 1976.

The National Physical Laboratory was established in 1900 in the grounds of Bushy House, where it has remained. In 1909 a fierce gale blew down many trees and once again, decades later in 1987, when more than 1,329 trees fell down in a hurricane which hit the park. It took more than three months to clear the fallen trees from the Waterhouse Woodland Gardens alone.

During the First World War, a large encampment of Canadian troops was stationed in Bushy Park. Several wooden buildings were erected in the grounds of Upper Lodge, which was used as the King's Canadian Hospital. Many Canadian soldiers who died of their wounds are buried in St James's Parish Church, Hampton Hill. From 1919 to the mid-1930s a residential open-air school for undernourished children, known as the King's Canadian Camp School, was located here. The totem pole and the Canadian glade in the Waterhouse Woodland Gardens are reminders of this connection.

How Bushy Park ended the Second World War

'You are about to embark upon the Great Crusade, toward which we have striven these many months. The eyes of the world are upon you. The hopes and prayers of liberty-loving people everywhere march with you,' were words by Dwight D. Eisenhower in 1944, and the role that Bushy Park played in this 'Great Crusade' should never be forgotten.

At the Casablanca conference in January 1943, Sir Winston Churchill, President Roosevelt and the Russian leader, Joseph Stalin, agreed to set up an Anglo-American group to plan the invasion of France and create a 'Second Front', led by the Chief of Staff to the Supreme Allied Commander, the British General Sir Frederick Morgan. By July 1943, the group had worked out the basics of what was to be the greatest invasion the world had known. In December 1943, General Dwight D. Eisenhower was appointed as Supreme Commander Allied Expeditionary Force, taking over the plans. Eisenhower was an unusual choice as he had no battle experience, but made up for this as he had a formidable grasp of the complexities of warfare with significant powers of diplomacy and political expertise.

Eisenhower disliked the headquarters at Grosvenor Square allocated to him by the British government and was keen to be free of the distractions of London. He sent his British aide, Colonel James Gault, to seek more suitable accommodation. Gault visited the HQ of General Spaatz's Eighth Air Force, at Bushy Park, which had been there since September 1942. Camp Griffiss was named after Lt Colonel Townsend Griffiss, an outstanding Eighth United States Army Air Force (USAAF) pilot killed in the European Theatre of Operations (ETO). He was shot down by mistake, while returning from a top secret trip to Russia, by a Polish RAF Spitfire pilot, in the Spring of 1942. What Griffiss' mission was or what he was flying has never been revealed.

When the site was acquired by the 8th USAAF as their headquarters, they took over buildings put up as emergency office accommodation after the destruction in London during the blitz. These temporary structures were to form the nucleus of Camp Griffiss. It received its codename of Widewing because of the wide wingspan of the legendary B-17 Flying Fortress, the main heavy bomber operated by the 8th USAAF. In general terms, USAAF personnel would call the American base Camp Griffiss, while members of Eisenhower's Supreme Headquarters Allied Expeditionary Forces (SHAEF) would always refer to it as Widewing. In January 1944, after reorganisation, it became the headquarters of General Carl Spaatz's United States Strategic Air Force in Europe (USSAFE), which included both the 8th and the Italian based 15th USAAFs.

Eisenhower officially moved into Camp Griffiss on 5 March 1944 despite the grumbling among his staff. The immense complex held 1,600 U.S. and 1,299 British personnel. It seemed the ideal site: not too near to London; much of the infrastructure such as communications, liaison, etc, was already in place; and significantly Eisenhower hoped that the proximity of Spaatz's headquarters would lead to informal cooperation. Incredibly, Eisenhower had no direct control over the Allied strategic air forces. He saw teamwork as crucial to the success of the invasion and had already appointed the British Air Marshal Tedder as Deputy Supreme Commander, whom he knew and respected from their time together in the Mediterranean Theatre a year earlier.

Gault had chosen a mansion on Kingston Hill for Eisenhower's personal accommodation, but Ike thought it too palatial and chose instead to take up residence in Telegraph Cottage, Kingston Hill. One of many air raids on Bushy occurred the night before Ike moved into his new headquarters. It was estimated that 1,000 incendiaries fell around the camp and started the rumour that the Nazis knew Eisenhower was moving in before he did.

Eisenhower's new HQ consisted of groups of huts and tents under dreary camouflage amid the vast cold expanse of Bushy Park and must have presented a drab picture after the hotels and night life of London for his staff. They set up in 'C' Block along a dimly lit corridor. The concrete floors were bare, and the offices cold and damp. The staff, including the Supreme Commander, were obliged to wear long socks and underwear to keep warm enough to work. Eisenhower felt this would help them visualise what the troops were to suffer during the winters to come in Europe. He thought that the conditions were ideal for concentrating on the enormous problems for the invasion. It may well have helped for it was remarked that the state of Camp Griffiss was such that the war had to be won quickly to avoid the total collapse of the buildings.

The site of Eisenhower's office along with the remains of Camp Griffiss were demolished in the early 1960s when the Americans finally vacated the site. His office was modest with a square desk with three flags on the top, his own four star general's flag and those of the USA and Great Britain. There were two buzzers, one to call his driver and the other summoned his personal secretary, Mattie Pinnette. He had two telephones on a table nearby, one of them his green 'scrambler' for secret conversations. Around him hung pictures of his wife, Mamie, his son, John, and his mother, Ida. There were also signed photographs of US President Roosevelt, Admiral Sir Andrew

Cunningham (First Sea Lord and Sir Winston Churchill's principal naval strategist), and General George C. Marshall, Chief of Staff. The walls also held secret maps which were locked behind silver screens when anyone under the rank of Lieutenant came into the room. A swivel chair, a couch and two armchairs completed the furnishings. Ike also needed to take rest and relaxation which he managed to do, partly through reading westerns and riding horses in Richmond Park, and on occasions, hand sketching, often drawing the pine trees he could see from his office window.

Meanwhile, Eisenhower assembled around himself and Tedder the team who were to improve General Morgan's invasion plans even further. It was Sir Winston Churchill who proposed the appointment of Admiral Bertram Ramsey to lead the predominantly British naval forces. Ramsey had commanded at Dunkirk and at the landing in North Africa and his experience would come in useful if things became difficult on the beaches.

General (later Field Marshal) Bernard L. Montgomery was designated commander of the ground forces – an appointment which was to prove fractious, as his constant disagreements with the American army commanders over strategy and tactics disrupted the close cooperation which Eisenhower considered vital for the smooth running of this team. Air Chief Marshal Trafford

Leigh-Mallory took command of the newly formed Allied Tactical Air Force, which comprised the British 2nd and the American 9th Air Forces. The plans and ideas of these men and their staff, hatched in this quiet spot of Bushy Park, were destined to write the pages of history and to secure the future of the free world. The success on the beaches is legendary and was the turning point of the Second World War. It did not, however, immediately signal the end of Bushy Park's association with Eisenhower. He kept his HQ at the park until SHAEF was relocated to Versailles on 20 September 1944.

The landscape structure of this part of Bushy Park still reflects, at a subtle level, the temporary occupation of the site. To many casual visitors this is just another part of the deer park. The presence, however, and alignments of Lombardy poplars and, to a lesser extent, horse chestnut and sycamore, are reminders of the former camp layout. It is a haunting experience to stand on the site of Eisenhower's office in the peace and tranquillity of Bushy Park and to try to imagine the momentous decisions which were taken and the events which occurred.

The Royal Parks have commemorated and interpreted this important historical site, whilst maintaining the ambience and natural beauty of the parkland. The SHAEF memorial was installed in 1994 on the 50th anniversary of SHAEF moving to Bushy Park. The plaque marks the

The SHAEF Memorial. © Peter Jeffree

position of Eisenhower's office and was designed by Epsom School of Art and Design. SHAEF Gate also commemorates D-Day and was installed in 1994. The gate marks the former main entrance to the camp used by SHAEF. A copse was also planted, imaginatively called D-Day Copse.

NOT TO BE MISSED ON A VISIT TO BUSHY PARK

Waterhouse Woodland Gardens

Along with the Diana fountain, a visit to the Waterhouse Woodland Gardens should be included, originally a woodland walk created in 1925, and consisting of two early nineteenth-century plantations. In 1948–9, improvements were carried out by the then park superintendent Joseph Fisher, who was responsible for the new paths and gardens that remain the backbone of the gardens today. A visitor centre and restaurant are present to serve the millions of visitors to this rural Royal Park.

Woodland Water Gardens. © Peter Jeffree

The Upper Lodge Water Gardens

One of the more interesting parts of Bushy Park, but often missed by many visitors, are the original water gardens which were built by Charles Montagu, the 1st Earl of Halifax, when he took over as ranger of the park early in 1709. The earl had been ambassador to the court of Hanover and allegedly he was inspired by the royal gardens he saw there – although the unusual three-lobed pool was copied from a pool built a few years earlier at Boughton House, Northamptonshire by his uncle John Montagu. Halifax exploited three different water sources in the park to create his baroque water gardens, which extended across the full width of the 'Upper' or 'Olde' Park.

He straightened the course of the Longford River from its entry into the park, routing it into the newly formed octagonal basin and over a cascade into the lower pool before returning to the river for its onward journey to Hampton Court Palace. Imitation grottoes were built as alcoves on each side of the cascade with seasonal backdrops painted on canvas inside them. Sadly, the earl did not live long to enjoy his new gardens. After his death in 1715 the gardens declined and were denuded for later developments in the park. The present Upper Lodge overlooking the water gardens was built around 1840, replacing the earl's original house of 1709. Part of the Crown Estate, it was a 'grace and favour' home until the early twentieth century.

The restored Upper Lodge Gardens, often missed by visitors to Bushy Park. © Peter Jeffree

Cascades of the Upper Lodge Water Gardens. © Peter Jeffree

In the early 1990s the Friends of Bushy Park became aware how much of the original water gardens remained beneath the former Admiralty research stations and began to explore options for their restoration. In 1994, the Admiralty released its lease back to the Crown Estate, who began tidying up the site. In 1995, the garden historian Jane Crawley had identified the water gardens in the background to *A Pair of Peafowl in a Park by an Ornamental Pond*, a painting by Jacob Bogdani (1660–1724) and, in 1999, Sir Roy Strong recognised the water gardens in the more detailed painting, *Cascade at Bushy Park* (1715), in the Royal Collection at Hampton Court. Other contemporary illustrations and accounts surfaced including John Rocque's *Bushy Park map of Upper Lodge* (1711) and an etching by Bernard Lens.

In 1997, the Friends group formed the Bushy Park Water Gardens Trust to restore the gardens and open them to the public. Supported by the Heritage Lottery Fund, the trust carried out extensive historical and archaeological work and, in partnership with the Crown Estate and the Royal Parks, developed a restoration plan. In 2001, the Royal Parks took the lead on the project and all works were completed by 2009.

A hidden gem at Bushy Park – the former Weirhouse and Totem pole

Tucked away by Waterhouse Pond is a former nineteenth century mess facility for the Longford Rivermen at the Waterhouse Pond known as the Weirhouse. Close by is also a totem pole, located north of the Waterhouse Pond in the Waterhouse Woodland Garden and installed to mark the connection between Canada and Bushy Park, which housed a large Canadian camp during the First World

The former Weirhouse. © David Bridges

Totem pole. © Gary Knight

War. The totem pole was donated with the assistance of the Canadian High Commission and designed by Nishga carver Norman Tait. At its base is 'Killerwhale', the monarch of the sea, and on top 'Eagle', the monarch of the air. They represent contact between Europeans and native Americans, first by sea and then by air.

INVOLVED WITH BUSHY PARK

Charles Montagu, 1st Earl of Halifax (1661–1715)

Charles Montagu, 1st Earl of Halifax, was a Whig statesman, as well as a financial genius who created several of the key elements of England's system of public finance. He was elected to Parliament in 1689 and appointed a Lord of the Treasury three years later. By devising a system of guaranteed government loans, Montagu financed British participation in the War of the Grand Alliance with France (1689–97) and initiated the national debt. With another set of loans he established the Bank of England in 1694. Shortly thereafter he became Chancellor of the Exchequer and a member of the small group of Whig leaders known as the Junto. Elected to parliament in 1695, he at once pushed through a controversial scheme of national recoinage. In 1697 he became first Lord of the Treasury and leader of the House of Commons. He resigned under pressure from a Tory-dominated Parliament in 1699, and in 1700 he was made Baron Halifax. When George I assumed the crown in 1714, Montagu was appointed first Lord of the Treasury and created an earl, but he died (without issue) after only seven months in office.

Halifax was also a minor poet and a literary patron; with Matthew Prior he wrote *The Country Mouse and the City Mouse* (1687), a witty parody of *The Hind and the Panther* by Dryden.

General Dwight D. Eisenhower (1890–1969)

Bringing to the presidency his prestige as commanding general of the victorious forces in Europe during the Second World War, Dwight D. Eisenhower obtained a truce in Korea and worked incessantly during his two terms to ease the tensions of the Cold War. He pursued the moderate policies of 'Modern Republicanism,' pointing out as he left office, 'America is today the strongest, most influential, and most productive nation in the world.'

Born in Texas in 1890, brought up in Abilene, Kansas, Eisenhower was the third of seven sons. He excelled in sports in high school, and received an appointment to West Point. Stationed in Texas as a second lieutenant, he met Mamie Geneva Doud, whom he married in 1916. In his early army career, he excelled in staff assignments, serving under Generals John J. Pershing, Douglas MacArthur, and Walter Krueger. After Pearl Harbor, General George C. Marshall called him to Washington for a war plans assignment. He commanded

Charles Montagu, 1st Earl of Halifax, 1732.
© Yale Center for British Art, Paul Mellon Collection

the Allied Forces landing in North Africa in November 1942; on D-Day, 1944, he was Supreme Commander of the troops invading France, and was based here in Bushy Park.

After the war, he became President of Columbia University, then took leave to assume supreme command over the new NATO forces being assembled in 1951. Republican emissaries to his headquarters near Paris persuaded him to run for president in 1952, winning a sweeping victory. Negotiating from military strength, he tried to reduce the strains of the Cold War. In 1953, the signing of a truce brought an armed peace along the border of South Korea. The death of Stalin the same year caused shifts in relations with Russia. New Russian leaders consented to a peace treaty that left Austria neutral. Meanwhile, both Russia

General Dwight D. Eisenhower addresses American paratroopers prior to D-Day. Unknown US Army photographer

and the United States had developed hydrogen bombs. With the threat of such destructive force hanging over the world, Eisenhower, with the leaders of the British, French, and Russian governments, met at Geneva in July 1955. The president proposed that the United States and Russia exchange blueprints of each other's military establishments and 'provide within our countries facilities for aerial photography to the other country.' The Russians greeted the proposal with silence, but were so cordial throughout the meetings that tensions relaxed.

Suddenly, in September 1955, Eisenhower suffered a heart attack in Denver, Colorado. After seven weeks he left the hospital, and in February 1956 doctors reported his recovery. In November he was elected for his second term. Eisenhower concentrated on maintaining world peace. Before he left office in January 1961 for his farm in Gettysburg, he urged the necessity of maintaining an adequate military strength, but cautioned that vast, long-continued military expenditures could breed potential dangers to our way of life. He concluded with a prayer for peace 'in the goodness of time.' Both themes remained timely and urgent when he died, after a long illness, on 28 March 1969.

4

ST JAMES'S PARK
A PARK OF GREAT MAJESTY

'St James's Park was not always so well-kempt and picturesque as it is today. It was once a swampy flat subject to flooding from the Thames and the Tyburn stream, the latter flowing through it.' Richard Church opens this as his description of St James's Park in his 1956 Guide Book, one of the busiest yet smallest of the Royal Parks. It has a huge history and has a great deal packed into its boundaries.

St James's Park well deserves its epithet of 'royal' surrounded as it is by three palaces. The most ancient is Westminster, which we now know as the Houses of Parliament. St James's Palace, its Tudor brickwork still intact, remains the official court, the 'court of St James's', although the monarch has lived at the third and most well-known one, Buckingham Palace, since 1837. A fourth palace, Whitehall, was burned down in 1698 and only Inigo Jones' fine Banqueting House remains.

The area now occupied by the park was once a marshy water meadow, subject to flooding from the Tyburn stream which flowed through it. In the thirteenth century a leper hospital dedicated to St James was founded for fourteen poor leprous maidens. It is from this hospital that the park took its name. Henry VIII acquired the site as a deer park in 1532 and built the Palace of St James alongside. The park was enclosed, and duelling, even the drawing of a sword, was forbidden within its bounds. Primarily a deer park with shooting butts, it included a bowling green, a tilt yard, tennis court, rural garden and a bathing pond. When Elizabeth I came to the throne she indulged her love of pageantry and pomp in the park. Fêtes of all kinds were held, but the park was wild and marshy and more suitable for the queen's frequent hunting parties than for jousts and tournaments. Her successor, James I, improved the drainage and controlled the water supply. He introduced a menagerie, with an elephant, crocodiles and other beasts – gifts from foreign princes. Birds, including pelicans donated by

Whitehall rooftops from St James's Park. © Peter Jeffree

the Russian ambassador, had already become an important part of the scene, for the king kept 'outlandish fowl' and had an aviary in the park – hence the name Birdcage Walk. At about this time a road was also created in front of St James's Palace, approximately where the Mall is today.

Although Charles I made minor improvements to the park, it was his son, Charles II, who on his restoration to the throne made significant changes. During his exile in France, the king came to admire many aspects of French court life, among them the formal gardens of André Le Nôtre at Versailles. On his return to England he wished for a similar formal layout in St James's. The park was redesigned, probably by André Mollet, with a rectangular ornamental canal about half a mile long running its length. Avenues of trees were planted and lawns laid out to be grazed by goats, sheep and deer. When it was finished the king opened the park to the public and he was a frequent visitor, feeding the ducks and mingling with his subjects.

During his exile in France, King Charles had also enjoyed playing

Pelicans in the park.

The Promenade in St James's Park, 1793.
© Yale Center for British Art, Paul Mellon Collection

paille-maille, an obsolete game resembling croquet. The names of the Mall and Pall Mall are derived from the court of pulverised cockleshells the king had made alongside the park. St James's Park served as a backcloth to many a Restoration comedy, a record of high society disporting itself in the park by day and by night. The collection of wildfowl dwindled after the death of Charles II, although William III took an interest in the duck decoy, a series of pools and channels designed to attract ducks. Storey's Gate is named after Edward Storey, the Keeper of the King's Birds. During William's reign the first tea house was built in the park. A regular Milk Fair was held around 1700 where different breeds of cow stood with their owners to provide fresh milk. For a while, it seemed like the park fell out of favour. There were strict regulations and it was locked at night but thousands had unofficial keys, and it became a noted haunt of whores of both sexes, often frequented by off duty soldiers at night. Indeed it was described as 'noxious to the health of the neighbouring inhabitations.'

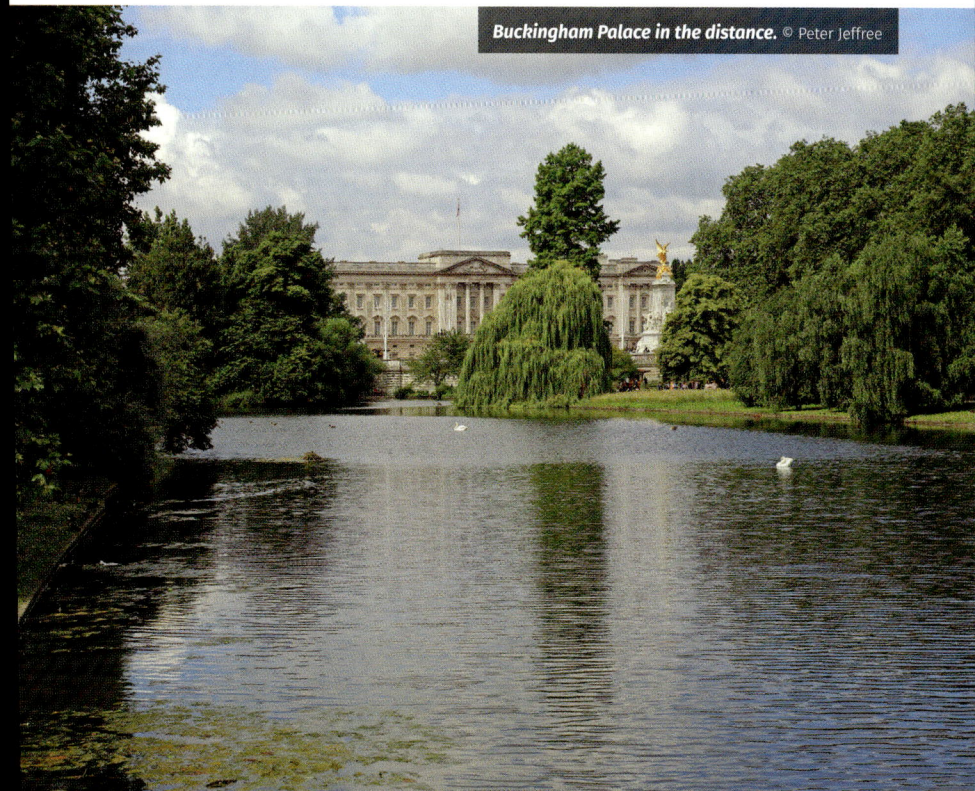

Buckingham Palace in the distance. © Peter Jeffree

The Chinese Pagoda and Bridge in St James's Park (previous to the fire), 1814. © Yale Center for British Art, Paul Mellon Collection

However, during the Hanoverian period improvements to the park were made. Horse Guards Parade was created by filling in one end of the long canal. From the formation of the Life Guards by Charles II, this space had been used first as a mustering ground and later for parades. Horse Guards Parade is very much part of St James's Park.

When the Duke of Buckingham built a house at the western end of the Mall, Queen Anne had not been pleased. It seemed as if both park and route had been created for the new house, leaving St James's Palace downgraded and off to one side. It was of course George III who bought Buckingham House in 1761

and his son, George IV, who built a new palace on the spot. Buckingham Palace with its extensive grounds stood at one end of a triumphal way, spanned by an arch, the Marble Arch (later moved to its present position on the edge of Hyde Park), and lined with grand residential terraces.

The park changed forever when architect John Nash redesigned it for the king. Begun in 1827, Nash carried out 'the best obliteration of avenues' – but it was also described as 'astounding ingenuity.' Nash created a park of more romantic style, removing all formality with the canal transformed into a natural looking lake, surrounded by winding paths and lawns studded with floriferous shrubberies and clumps of trees. This English style of gardening, as it came to be known, was the inspiration of Humphry Repton and Capability Brown. Like many of the other Royal Parks, St James's Park was used for celebration. National celebrations such as the defeat of Napoleon and the Glorious Peace of 1814 ended in tragedy when a tall Chinese pagoda was consumed by flames with the loss of several lives. In 1837 the Ornithological Society of London presented some birds to the park and erected a cottage for a bird keeper on Duck Island.

For many years, with increased public access, the park moved through the seasons with little change. Then, during the Second World War, the lake was drained, its bed covered with bungalows to serve as extra offices and a canteen for the overflow of work and staff from government departments. The park was restored soon after the war and today it is a regular destination for visitors and office workers alike, making it the most popular of all the Royal Parks.

NOT TO BE MISSED ON A VISIT TO ST JAMES'S PARK

Duck Island Cottage

St James's Park has so much to offer to the visitor, with buildings, monuments and facilities for all. Of them all, Duck Island Cottage is possibly the most picturesque. It is more than aptly named as it occupies a site which has long been the haunt of many aquatic birds. Birds of various kinds have been kept here since 1612, when James I began converting the swampy chase of the Tudor monarchs into a formal garden. Here, along what is now Birdcage Walk, an aviary was established and native and foreign waterfowl found refuge in the park.

It was in 1837 that the Ornithological Society of London was founded to protect the birds and undertook to form and maintain a complete collection of Water Fowl – swimmers, divers and waders kept, as nearly as possible, in a natural state. The society appealed for support not 'to the scientific alone' but to 'all persons who are capable of appreciating the charm which the presence of the feather tribes lends to ornamental water'. The society enjoyed the patronage of Prince Albert of Saxe-Coburg & Gotha and its printed prospectus is garnished with the names of its noble and distinguished supporters. The membership was small and select – a fact ensured by an expensive subscription.

It was in 1840 that the society submitted a 'Memorial' to the commissioners seeking permission to build a house for a bird-keeper in St James's Park and made a grant of £300 towards the cost of its construction. The commissioned architect was John Burges Watson who had been engaged by the society to design the bird keeper's cottage. Watson was an obscure architect whose 'taste was for rural subjects'. He produced a small, irregular composition, comprising a cottage and clubroom for the society, trimmed with ornamental barge-boards, finials and ridge-tiles. The cottage was proposed to occupy Duck Island while the clubroom was to stand on a small promontory on the nearby bank, the two buildings connected by a loggia-like bridge of tree-trunk columns and trellis, beneath which water flowed. This gingerbread *Cottage Orné*, of vaguely Swiss inspiration, was calculated to contrast with the increasingly monumental and grandiose architecture of the government offices being erected in nearby Whitehall.

Sadly, the new society languished and did little on Duck Island and the cottage slid gently into obscurity. By 1953, the cottage was deemed to be unfit for human habitation and was eventually abandoned. Duck Island Cottage seemed doomed. Demolition seemed inevitable but, on account of it being 'so much in the public eye', it was agreed that the Royal Fine Art Commission should be consulted before its potential destruction. At the same time, designs were being sought for a

Duck Island Cottage. © Peter Jeffree

replacement cottage. The commission intervened and urged the preservation of Duck Island Cottage, leading to the retention of the building.

In 1959, it was vigorously re-modelled and extended and once more given over to habitation. Coated in pebble-dash and shorn of most of its ornaments, the cottage provided an utilitarian home to two spinster park keepers who lived there until 1980. It was only in 1982 that Duck Island Cottage was carefully restored, the later additions removed and its full amount and number of decorative features reinstated – including the distinctive lozenge-latticed glazing bars. The channel of water beneath the rustic loggia, absent since its suppression in 1882, was also reinstated. After briefly serving as an office for the bird keeper and as a store for confiscated bicycles, Duck Island Cottage was allocated as the temporary headquarters of the London Historic Parks and Gardens Trust in 1994. Today, it is more than appropriate that Duck Island Cottage has been bestowed upon the trust – a society concerned with the protection and enhancement of St James's Park. However, the philanthropic and didactic objectives of the trust extend beyond the boundaries of the Mall and Birdcage Walk. They encompass parks and gardens throughout London – all historic pleasure grounds which, like St James's Park, continue to provide enjoyment and benefit for the residents and visitors to the metropolis.

The Inn on the Park

The Inn on the Park restaurant replaces the original cake house that was designed by Eric Bedford and opened by Mrs Harold Wilson in 1970. St James's Park has been associated with refreshments for many years, dating back as far as 1666 when milk fairs were established. In the eighteenth century cows were tethered and milked on the spot, the milk served 'with all the cleanliness peculiar to the English, in little mugs at the rate of 1d per mug'.

In 1998, plans for a new cake house were unveiled but with it came controversy. The Royal Fine Art Commission slammed the plan by one of its own commissioners, Sir Michael Hopkins, to build a new cake house it considered 'wholly unsuited' to the proposed site in St James's Park. The £1.6 million 'environmentally friendly' scheme was branded 'typically elegant' by then arts minister Mark Fisher. Hopkins' scheme had attempted to enhance the landscape by 'following more closely Nash's original landscape intentions' through rolling over the building a gently curved green roof, planted with ground cover. But the commission's chairman Lord St John of Fawsley had many concerns about the project, the most important of which was its size. He argued that pavilions such as the previous cake house were needed because of the *rus in urbe* ('country in the city') nature of the Grade

The Inn on the Park. © Peter Jeffree

I-listed park, and that he was 'unhappy' about the visibility of the building, especially the walkway and balustrade.

Described by Hopkins' architects, 'at a point where two sweeping paths meet, a double curved, lozenge shaped space is created, set within a gently rising hillock. The surrounding grass landscape rolls up on to a roof top terrace. Approaching from all sides, the café emerges as an elegant wood clad shelter, with a glazed frontage, making full use of the spectacular views'.

Horse Guards Parade

Horse Guards Parade was once the site of Henry VIII's tiltyard but has been a parade ground since the late seventeenth century. The Horse Guards building was designed by William Kent who retained and incorporated the clock turret from the old Horse Guards on the site. Facing the barracks is the Guards Memorial which was installed in memory of guardsmen who died in the First World War and unveiled in 1926 by the Duke of Connaught, the uncle of King George V. It was designed by H. Chalton Bradshaw with sculpture by Gilbert Ledward. After the Second World War, an inscription was added to remember those who died between 1939 and 1945. The sculptures were made from guns captured in the First World War and modelled on real guardsmen, representing Grenadier, Coldstream, Scots, Irish and Welsh guards. The Irish

Horse Guards Parade. © Peter Jeffree

The Guards Memorial, unveiled in 1926.

guardsman got impatient while he was being modelled and left before the artist had finished, so his legs belong to another soldier. The memorial was damaged by German bombs during the Second World War and during the repairs a small hole was deliberately left in one of the sculptures.

Monuments of St James's Park

St James's Park has many other monuments within and surrounding the park, including the Boy statue, just off Birdcage Walk and which was designed by Charles Henry Mabey, and the Bali Memorial, one of the many monuments found around the perimeter and outskirts of the park. It commemorates the 202 victims of the Bali bombings in 2002 and is located at Clive Steps, along Horse Guards Road, and within view of Duck Island Cottage. Others include the Royal Naval Division Memorial and is dedicated to the 45,000 members of the Royal Naval Division who died or were wounded during the First World War, and is located next to Old Admiralty

The Bali Memorial. © Peter Jeffree

buildings in the north-west corner of Horse Guards Parade. One of the more unusual monuments is known as the Regent's Bomb, in the style of a Chinese dragon, also known as the Cadiz Memorial and was captured at the battle of Salamanca and was presented by Spain to mark the lifting of the siege of Cadiz in 1812 by Wellington.

The most impressive monument overlooking the park though is the one celebrating the Duke of York which was installed in memory of Frederick William (1763–1827), Commander-in-Chief of the British army and second son of King George III. The statue was designed by Sir Richard Westmacott in 1834. The 124 feet Tuscan column was designed by Benjamin Wyatt. The Duke of York was a highly proficient Commander-in-Chief whose administrative reforms won the

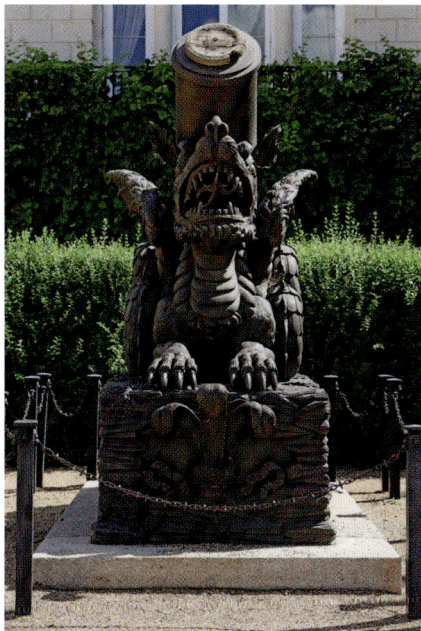

The Cadiz Memorial. © Peter Jeffree

The Duke of York overlooking St James's Park. © Peter Jeffree

praise of Wellington. Unfortunately, he was less successful in his private life. The revelation that his mistress, Mary Anne Clarke, was selling commissions forced his resignation. Although he was reinstated, he died in debt. It was claimed that he was placed on a column to avoid the claims of his creditors. The monument cost £21,000 and much of it was raised by soldiers who donated a day's pay.

A hidden gem at St James's Park – Storey's Gate

Unlike many of the other Royal Parks, there is only one remaining lodge in St James's Park. Storey's Gate Lodge sits on the corner of Birdcage Walk and Horse Guards Road with Big Ben in the background. It is built of stock brick with Portland stone dressings, and a slate roof. Described as functional, yet plain neo-classicism, it is one storey on a rectangular plan with a stone doorcase of Doric pilasters, entablature and blocking course. 'Storey's Gate' was named after Edward Storey, Keeper of the King's Birds, whose house is believed to have stood nearby.

Storey's Gate. © Peter Jeffree

André Mollet (1600–1665)

André Mollet was a French garden designer and writer active in England, as royal gardener to both Charles I and II, in the seventeenth century. Mollet came from a family of gardeners and is especially noted for writing the highly influential *Le Jardin de plaisir* (1651).

Mollet became royal gardener to Queen Christina in Stockholm. His lasting record is his handsomely-printed folio, *Le Jardin de plaisir* (*The Pleasure Garden*), published in Stockholm in 1651, which he illustrated with meticulous copperplate engravings after his own designs, and which, with an eye to a European aristocratic clientele, he published in Swedish, French and German. In his designs the rich patterning of parterres, which had formerly been a garden feature of interest in isolation, was for the first time arranged in significant relation to the plan of the house. Mollet's designs coordinated the elements of scythed turf with gravel paths, basins and fountains, parterres, *bosquets* and *allées*.

Mollet was summoned to England in the 1620s to lay out gardens for Charles I and perhaps the parterres at Wilton House, but by 1633 he was in the service of Prince Frederick Henry of Orange.

Mollet received a passport to travel abroad once more in 1653 to London. With the English Restoration in 1660, conditions for ambitious garden-building were once more propitious, and Mollet was listed as a royal gardener, gardener-in-chief for St James's Park. An English edition of *Le Jardin de plaisir* appeared in London in 1670, as *The Pleasure Garden*.

5

GREEN PARK
A PARK OF SIMPLE BEAUTY

Richard Church acknowledges that Green Park is 'quite different in character' to all the other Royal Parks, describing the trees as 'luxuriant, their heavy foliage hanging nearly to the ground, so that one walks there with one's personality reduced to "a green thought in a green shade." It is a restful process for tired nerves.'

Set in a stunning location between Piccadilly and Constitution Hill, with Buckingham Palace and the Victoria memorial gardens beyond, and at its eastern boundary, the Queen's Walk, running down from the Ritz hotel to Lancaster House in the Mall, there would appear to be a lot to get excited about Green Park. But actually, little has happened here over its many years.

When Charles II returned from Europe and reclaimed his throne, the ground between the wall of St James's Palace and what ultimately became known as Piccadilly was waste ground and meadow. Two shallow hills were planted with a few willow trees, and the ground was crossed by a variety of ditches. It was Charles who enclosed at least 36 acres with a high brick wall; the land within became known as Upper St James's Park, and it was here he set up a deer harbour. Another 41 acres were added to the west. Avenues of trees were planted, and formal gravelled paths were laid down and a ranger's lodge was built for the official in charge. In the centre of this new park, Charles II built a 'snow house and an ice-house, as the mode is in some parts of France and Italy, and other hot countries, for to cool wines and other drinks for the summer season.'

Several new houses were also built on St James's Fields, which bordered the park on the east, and along Piccadilly, to the north, several grand mansions appeared. There were, however, significant differences between Upper St James's Park and Lower St James's Park. In the Upper Park, there were no restrictions on 'sword-drawing' so it became a favourite resort for duels.

The eighteenth century saw many further improvements to Upper St James's Park. At the north-east end a canal or reservoir was excavated, which was enlarged in 1730 to enable the Chelsea Water Company to provide for the growing needs of St James's Palace, the park and Buckingham House. The reservoir was embellished with a lively but decorative fountain, which became known as 'The Queen's Basin' at around the same time as 'The Queen's Walk' was being laid out along the eastern boundary. Queen Caroline, wife of George II, had been making many improvements around the palace at Kensington and took great interest in Upper St James's Park and gave orders for the preparation of a private walk so that members of the royal family might divert themselves there in the spring, without being too much disturbed by the general public. At the Mall end she had built, to designs by William Kent, 'The Queen's Library' – in reality this was nothing more than a summerhouse overlooking the park.

Throughout the century, the park was to witness many military parades and manoeuvres, especially intense during the most critical periods of the War of Austrian Succession (1740–48). When the war was brought to an end through the Treaty of Aix-la-Chapelle, George was to witness from an ornate pavilion specially built near the Queen's Library the spectacular celebrations in the park to commemorate this event. The building was called the Temple of Peace and was designed by Msgr Cavalieri Servadoni,

who had a significant reputation in Paris. The building would be fitted, at its centre, with a 'grand and extensive' musical gallery, above which would be an allegorical figure of 'Peace' attended by the massive figures of Neptune and Mars. On a pole at the top was to be an illumination representing the sun, which was to burn, allegedly, almost throughout the night of festivities. Handel was chosen to compose a grand military overture, with over one hundred cannon fired from arcades in the temple to provide the punctuation. Apart from the royal pavilion there were comfortable viewing galleries for the Privy Council, the House of Lords, the House of Commons, foreign diplomats and the dignitaries of the City of London, led by the lord mayor.

Beyond all these enclosures for the most privileged, great crowds of people milled about. All the park gates had been opened and there was a long gap in the wall facing Piccadilly to facilitate entrance. As soon as the king was in his place, the performance started with Handel's great overture, cannons firing when disaster struck. The Temple of Peace caught fire, and in the ensuing minutes Upper St James's Park became a scene of the most appalling confusion with many injuries and at least one fatality. With terrifying rapidity, the entire area became engulfed in a series of fires and explosions as thousands of fireworks were prematurely set alight. Within the privileged enclosures, panic also set in,

A Perspective View of the Building for the Fireworks in the Green Park, Taken from the Reservoir, 1749.
© Yale Center for British Art, Yale Art Gallery Collection

with the galleries being flimsily built and ornately draped. Royalty was forced to retreat, which was just as well, as the Queen's Library also caught fire and was badly damaged. Sadly, the Temple of Peace had not lasted long.

Further changes were made to Upper St James's Park during the latter part of the eighteenth century. In 1767, the park was reduced in size by George III so that the gardens of Buckingham House could be enlarged, and after 1780, the park was used less and less by the military and was increasingly used for social gathering. Lower St James's Park had deteriorated considerably and the Upper Park was seen as more fashionable, particularly due to the new houses north of Piccadilly.

With the apparent ending of the Napoleonic wars in the spring of 1814, the park was again chosen as one of the principal sites for a major national rejoicing. The beginning of August 1814 marked the centenary of the accession of the House of Hanover in England, so it was decided to combine the two celebrations, even though the Prince Regent was now so unpopular in London that the streets had often to be cleared before he drove out from his palace at Carlton House. On this occasion, nearly a third of the park from Constitution Hill downwards was taken over and an imaginative design for the temporary buildings was to be the background for a grand pyrotechnic display. The building, designed by

The Grand Pavilion in the Green Park. © Yale Center for British Art, Paul Mellon Collection

Sir William Congreve and plainly an emblem of war, was given the name the Temple of Concord, which suggested that some major transformation would take place in it before the celebrations were over. The entire structure slowly revolved so that the spectators could view all the scenes painted on the castle walls, which recalled the great heroes and triumphs of the British people, culminating in the victory over Napoleon. This was the first stage of the celebrations and was to be illuminated by the massed display of fireworks and the roar of cannon. On the very same evening, commemorations were under way in Lower St James's Park with elaborate celebrations designed by Nash. At midnight, the great fortress in Upper St James's Park revolved merrily on its axis with a deafening roar, and the celebrations went off without mishap – unlike in nearby Lower St James's Park. Many of those attending the upper park celebrations went down to the lower park in order to witness the chaos and mayhem there.

By the early 1820s both Green Park and St James's Park had deteriorated to such an extent that the Commissioners of Woods, the officials responsible for them, issued a strong report urging radical changes, which coincided with the wish of George IV and the government that both parks should in future be opened 'For the gratification and enjoyment of the Public'. In St James's Park this ultimately led to the Nash redevelopment previously described. In Green Park, suggestions were much less radical with the commissioners proposing the planting of shrubberies along the northern and eastern boundaries together with new plantations of trees.

After the death of George IV, William IV showed little interest and Green Park was sadly neglected. In 1835, a writer in *The Original* complained bitterly about the disgraceful state into which Green Park had been allowed to fall. There had been talk of terraced ornamental gardens being introduced to give beauty and grandeur to the vista stretching across the park to the palace as suggested by Sir Charles Barry, architect of the new Houses of Parliament, but nothing came of it. With the death of William, and with Queen Victoria now firmly ensconced in Buckingham Palace, Green Park was now well looked after within a landscape of trees, grass and paths. The Queen's Basin with its fountain had outlived its usefulness and was filled in. The decrepit ranger's lodge that had stood at the Hyde Park Corner end of the park was also demolished.

In the early years of Victoria's reign, a number of bizarre incidents occurred in or near Green Park. In June 1838, the female balloonist Mrs Graham was engaged by the government to make an ascent from Green Park as part of the queen's coronation festivities. This, however, ended in tragedy when one of the balloon's grapnels tore one of the coping stones from the roof of a house in Marylebone Lane which fatally hit a passer-by. In June 1840, an insane individual called Edward Oxford fired two shots at the young queen as she was driving past in her carriage with Prince Albert. A further attempt was made in May 1842 by another insane person named Francis, and yet another in 1849.

In essence, despite these traumatic and violent dramas throughout its history, Green Park has quietly changed with the seasons with some impressive additions. In 1889, the roadway at Constitution Hill was thrown open to the public as a thoroughfare for carriages, but limited to a number of specially favoured persons. In the early part of the twentieth century, the Broad Walk was given a more formal appearance as part of a vista from Piccadilly down through the park to the ornamental gates presented by the then Dominion of Canada. These led to the gardens around the massive statue of Queen Victoria in front of Buckingham Palace, unveiled by George V in 1911. The northern end of the vista was

Countryside within the city. © Peter Jeffree

greatly enriched in 1921 when the magnificent iron gates that had stood guard over Devonshire House on the north side of Piccadilly were bought from the then Duke of Devonshire who had sold the family town-house for redevelopment.

The Green Park that emerged from the nineteenth century and developed during the twentieth century is now a pleasantly uncluttered place, somewhat resembling a small expanse of countryside in the heart of our great capital city.

NOT TO BE MISSED ON A VISIT TO GREEN PARK

Green Park is now largely devoid of buildings and has very few monuments or artefacts, apart from a small number of recent introductions. Little has changed in the last century with few additions including the Constance Fund fountain with Diana the naked huntress, positioned in 1954, and the Canadian war memorial in 1994. These have not affected the atmosphere of the park and the only real hint of formality is provided by the Broad Walk and the ornamental iron gates at either end. It really is a park of very simple beauty.

The Constance Fund Fountain. © Peter Jeffree

A common sight in Green Park. © Peter Jeffree

Green Park and a green oasis in the heart of the city. © Peter Jeffree

Despite its simplicity, there is one element of Green Park that surpasses many of the others and that is the majesty of its entrances. These include the Dominion Gates, the Devonshire Gates and the Commonwealth Memorial Gates.

Green Park's Gates

Erected in 1908 in association with Sir Aston Webb's layout for the nearby Queen Victoria memorial, the Dominion Gates were presented by the dominions of Canada and Australia. Canada Gate is on the Green Park boundary; South and West Africa Gate (columns only) are on the Mall; and Australia Gate (columns and side gates only) on the south side; with outer columns for Newfoundland (north) and the Malay States (south). The Devonshire Gates date from 1735 and are much travelled and were designed by ironsmith Warren for Lord Heathfield's house at Turnham Green. They were then acquired by Lord Devonshire in 1837 for Chiswick House, erected at Devonshire House in 1898, and eventually purchased and erected on the present site in 1921. Inaugurated by Queen Elizabeth II in 2002 and designed by Liam O'Connor, the Commonwealth Memorial Gates consist of four pillars of Portland stone carved with the names India, Pakistan, Bangladesh, Sri Lanka, Africa, Caribbean and Kingdom of Nepal.

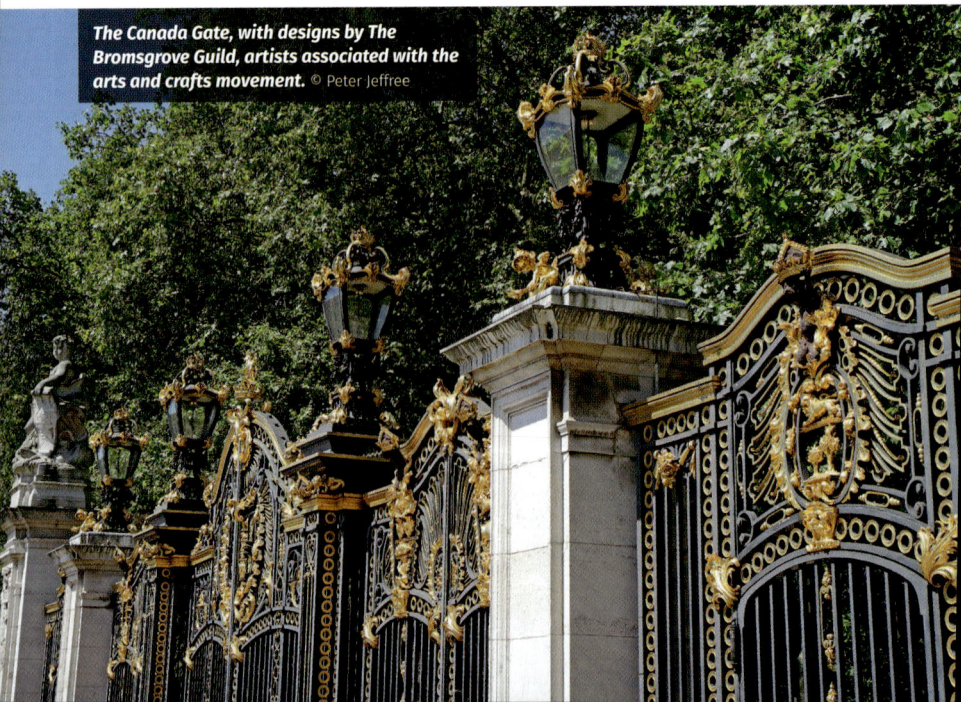

The Canada Gate, with designs by The Bromsgrove Guild, artists associated with the arts and crafts movement. © Peter Jeffree

The Devonshire Gates. © Peter Jeffree

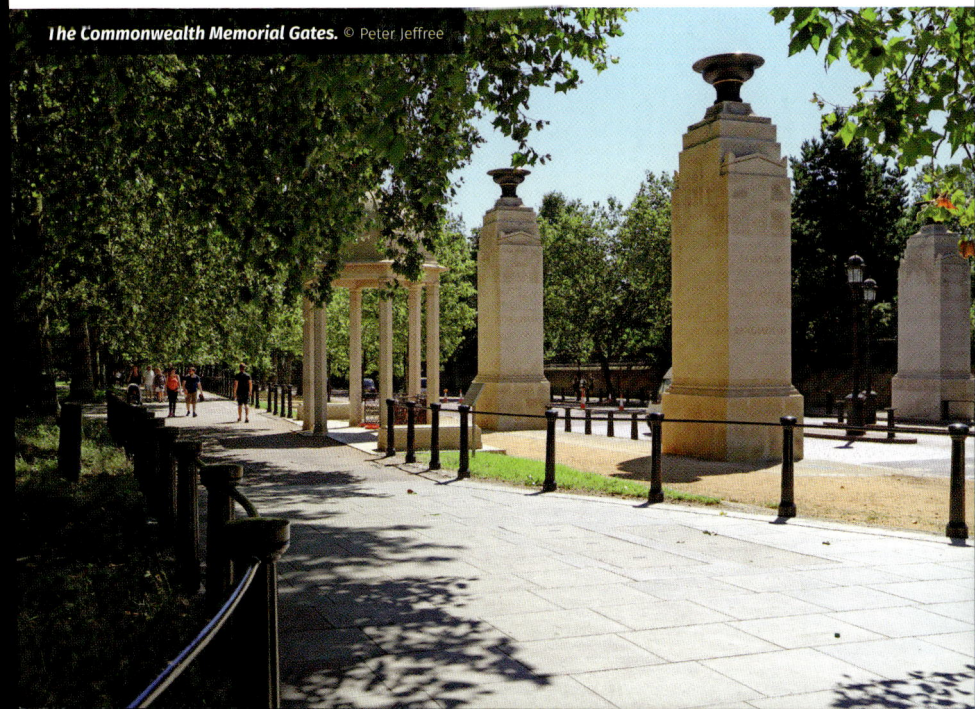

The Commonwealth Memorial Gates. © Peter Jeffree

Between the piers are a domed pavilion and two stone benches, located at the north-west end of Constitution Hill at the junction with Hyde Park Corner. This was the first permanent national recognition of the contribution and sacrifice made in the two world wars by nearly five million people from the Indian Sub-Continent, Africa and the Caribbean. The pillars are topped with a bronze urn and gas flames, which are lit on special occasions such as Remembrance Sunday, Armistice Day and Commonwealth Day. The names of holders of Victoria and George Crosses are engraved on the inside of the pavilion and the major campaigns are listed on the benches.

Bomber Command Memorial

Now located in Green Park, the Bomber Command Memorial has been built to be modern, yet classical, and in the Portland stone used elsewhere in the park. It came about as a result of a campaign mounted by *The Daily Telegraph* and *Daily Express*, along with veterans and others. At the heart of the memorial are the bronze sculptures of a Bomber Command aircrew. Within the memorial, the space is carefully designed and is open to the sky to allow light to fall directly onto sculptures of the aircrew below.

The scale of the sculpture is deliberate. Designed as a whole, it means that visitors will always see the profile of

Bomber Command Memorial and members of the aircrew. © Peter Jeffree

the total sculpture against the sky above them, both day and night, ensuring that section of the sky is powerfully symbolic for this stunning memorial. The design for the roof also incorporates sections of aluminium recovered from a Handley Page Halifax III bomber (LW682 from No. 426 Squadron) shot down over Belgium on the night of 12 May 1944, in which eight crew were killed. Three members of the crew were still at their stations when the aircraft was excavated in 1997. They were buried in Belgium with full military honours alongside the five other members of the crew. The memorial was officially unveiled by Queen Elizabeth II on 28 June 2012.

Yet, the memorial is not without controversy, described by author Andrew Jones in 2020 as 'hideous... terrible... without purpose... profoundly depressing'. He likens it to 'spooky Soviet realism'. From its outset it was strongly opposed by residents and heritage and garden conservation societies. Sadly it is frequently defaced by opposition groups and individuals who see such an edifice unsavoury, with Bomber Command a challenging cause to celebrate considering the mass destruction and loss of lives in Dresden, Lübeck and many other towns and cities in Germany. Jones is perhaps a little harsh, as the structure is a memorial to the airmen who gave their lives and despite the loss of so many lives, without their contributions, many more thousands could have perished.

A hidden gem at Green Park – Watering Holes

A unique sculptural stone fountain was launched in Green Park in 2012. This and 'Trumpet', another drinking fountain, were the winners of an international design competition supported by Tiffany & Co. Foundation, New York. Robin Monotti architects and Mark Titman's 'Watering Holes' is an impressive 800 kilograms slab of Cornish granite perforated with three watering holes at heights from which adults, children, wheelchair users and dogs can drink cool, fresh water, in one of London's most visited Royal Parks. The installation here in Green Park, near the new Bomber Command Memorial, was a two-year collaboration between the Royal Parks foundation, the Tiffany & Co. Foundation, as well as the Royal Parks and the Royal Institute of British Architects to create a new drinking fountain that is not only beautiful, but robust and which enhances

The Watering Holes drinking fountain – a contemporary sculpture in Green Park. © Peter Jeffree

the Royal Parks' Grade I listed landscape. The design competition attracted over 169 entries from twenty-six countries, and was an important element of 'Tiffany – Across the Water', a wider programme to restore drinking and ornamental fountains across the 5,000 acres of London's Royal Parks with the support of The Tiffany & Co. Foundation in New York.

INVOLVED WITH GREEN PARK

Edward Oxford

Queen Victoria was one of the country's most loved monarchs and our longest-reigning until Elizabeth II. However, she was not always popular and on one occasion, this nearly cost the queen her life.

Times were challenging for Victoria in 1840, as a young queen. She had married a man that many of her people disliked and a series of scandals meant opinion of Victoria was very mixed. She was already a strong-willed woman but she lacked experience, and relied heavily on her Prime Minister. She was also a little unsure of how to appeal to the common people. One of these common people was Edward Oxford, a handsome 18-year-old man with dark eyes and auburn hair. He had been hired as a pot boy at a local public house but was sacked after his laugh, often described as 'maniacal', disturbed too many of its customers. He was perceived as being a little peculiar ever since childhood, but grew up with a violent, drunken and often absent father. The young boy would often fly into fierce rages of his own, destroying everything in sight. Although he was bright and intelligent, he found school challenging and was so unpredictable at home, his mother had to confine the child to the cellar of her pastry shop so that he could not disturb the customers.

By the time he was a youth, he was angry and frustrated and had become a senior member of a secret society of like-minded angry youths known as 'young England'. He never seemed to settle into a single job and always felt that he was destined for more, and the last firing had been the final straw. He was determined for the world to see him as more than just a pot boy. He knew just how to go about this – he would plan to assassinate the young queen. Using the last of his wages he bought two pistols, powder and shot,

then spent several days practising at shooting galleries across the capital.

On 10 June he dressed smartly in a light silk waistcoat and brown frock coat and set off at a brisk walk towards the palace. When he reached it he found crowds of people jostling for a glimpse of the queen, so he passed through the entrance and continued along Constitution Hill. He picked his spot which was not too secluded and waited, leaning back against the iron railings of Green Park. Two hours later the immediate sound of cheering alerted him to the presence of the monarch. The queen, with the prince by her side, emerged from the garden gate in a tantalisingly open carriage pulled by four horses. As they waved to the crowd, Edward made his move. He walked forward, nodding his head, then drew a pistol from his coat. At just six paces away from the queen, he fired. Screams rang out among the crowd but the queen was unaffected; she wasn't even aware that she had been shot at. The horses started and the carriage came to an abrupt stop. Albert took his wife's hand in his and asked if the fright had shaken her, but she merely laughed in reply.

Knowing he had moments before he was spotted, Edward drew out his second pistol, but in the brief pause the queen had spotted him. She ducked as Albert pulled her down and Edward fired. The ball passed just above her head and stuck in the opposite wall, and in a moment the carriage rode away at speed. By the time the authorities reached the scene the angry crowd were chanting 'Kill him! Kill him!' But when the constable grabbed Edward by the collar he calmly commented: 'You have no occasion to use violence. I am the person. I will go quietly.'

When his case came before the courts, Edward was found not guilty on the grounds of insanity, then transferred to a mental hospital. He soon became a model patient, and was later released on the assurance that he would emigrate and never return to the country. Edward agreed, travelling to Australia, changing his name and finding employment as a housepainter.

Thanks to his reinvention he was able to climb the social ladder and was even invited as the guest of the Governor to the queen's 70th birthday celebrations. Now a gentleman of repute, he wrote to one of the few people who knew his true identity: 'I should like a certain illustrious lady to know that one who was a foolish boy half a century ago is now a respectable and respected member of society.'

The queen received an unexpected boon as a result of the assassination attempt. Iron willed, she insisted they continue with their outing despite the attempt at her life and returned to cheering crowds outside the palace. For the following days the royal couple were applauded everywhere they went, and there were even instances of the crowd randomly bursting into renditions of *God Save The Queen*. Edward Oxford had attempted to kill her, but in reality he had helped her gain exactly the popularity boost that she needed. 'It is worth being shot at to see how much one is loved' – Queen Victoria, 1882.

Edward Oxford shooting at Queen Victoria, 10 June 1840; the Queen and Prince Consort driving in a phaeton with four horses towards Constitution Hill; Oxford standing in front of the Green Park railings pointing a pistol in an attempt to assassinate the Queen, while a policeman runs towards him, one of the Queen's attendants on horse at left. By G. H. Miles

6

RICHMOND PARK
A MEDIEVAL ROYAL PASTURE

Our friend Richard Church clearly has a soft spot for Richmond Park, and who can blame him. He writes of 'the solitude, the atmosphere of old England, the spacious dignity... Richmond Park is a great repository of history, and especially royal history, the tale of our kings and queens, and the part they have played in the growth of our democratic way of life.' He isn't wrong. To many, it is the most magnificent of all the Royal Parks, and I would readily agree. On my every visit, I am astounded not just by its mere existence, but also the scale of the park and all that lies within it.

Royal connections go back at least to the days of Edward I (1272–1307) when the area was known as the Manor of Sheen. It was not until Henry VII came to the throne that the name was changed to Richmond by the king, after his earldom in Yorkshire. King Henry frequently stayed at Richmond Palace on the Thames, and had it rebuilt in a grander style after the original burned down. During his reign, and probably long before, much of what is now Richmond Park was a hunting ground known as Sheen Chase. His son, Henry VIII, also favoured Richmond Palace and the hunt, as did Elizabeth I who died in the palace.

In 1625 Charles I moved with his court to Richmond to escape the plague in London. He was 'excessively affected to hunting and the sports of the field' and 'had a great desire to make a great park for red as well as fallow deer between Richmond and Hampton Court'. The first known transaction from this period was a warrant dated 1630 'to prepare a bill for His Majesty's signature for payment of an imprest to Edward Manning for railing in coppices, making ponds, cutting lawns in the New Park at Richmond, and bringing a river to run through the same.' Payments were also made to Mr Manning to build a brick wall, completed by 1637 and measuring almost eight miles.

Charles I had created the park by force and enclosed it despite much opposition. This came, in particular, from those whose farms and estates the king insisted on purchasing and from the local country people, much of whose common land he took – although the price paid in compensation was considered fair. Perhaps as a concession, King Charles allowed pedestrians the right of way through the park and placed gates wherever the wall crossed a thoroughfare and ladders over the walls to retain access to the footpaths. He also stipulated that poor people should be allowed to carry away fallen deadwood from trees for firewood just as they had done before the enclosure.

During the Commonwealth (1649–60), Oliver Cromwell presented the park to the City of London in recognition of support given to his cause during the Civil War. The City's plan to profit from the park was stopped short by a statement from the House of Commons that the park 'should be preserved as a park, still without destruction...' On the restoration of the monarchy Charles II arrived in London in June 1660 to be met by the Lord Mayor of London and the City officers. Anxious to curry favour, they came 'to congratulate his Majesty's restoration and likewise to present the Newe Park to his Majestye...'

Between 1660 and 1667 Charles II spent over £3,000 on repairs to the walls, lodges and the 'Great Pond Head'. Later, from 1673 to 1683, permits were issued for the removal of 7,200 loads of gravel and the resulting pits formed the twenty five or so ponds around the park. Although William III came occasionally to shoot, his wife, Mary II, allowed the public to use the park other than as a right of way.

A royal presence in the park was re-established with George I who was responsible for the White Lodge. Begun in 1727, this hunting lodge was finished two years later under George II. The new king appointed Robert, Lord Walpole, son of Prime Minister Sir Robert Walpole, as ranger. During Walpole's rangership there were increased restrictions on public entry when the stiles were removed and lodges built at the gates. George II's daughter, Princess Amelia, succeeded Lord Walpole as ranger in 1751 and held the position until her resignation in 1761. She was a 'fanatical huntress' who did her best to exclude the public completely by ordering that all the foot-gates be closed. A test case was brought by John Lewis, a local brewer, against a gatekeeper who refused him entry to the park. Lewis won his case which was based on the rights for pedestrians granted by Charles I. At the trial the Assize Judge ruled that ladderstiles (which could not be locked) and gates be erected at East Sheen Gate and Ham Gate. When these entrances were opened 'a vast concourse of people from all the neighbouring villages climbed over the ladderstiles and into the park.' This victory by the people was a turning point in the history of the park. The days of 'the chase' were over and the public had established rights of access in law.

In 1788 a molecatcher's house in the west of the park was altered and improved by the eminent architect Sir John Soane for Elizabeth, Countess of Pembroke. Over the following 40 years, the countess made further additions to the building, known henceforth as Pembroke Lodge. George III himself was ranger between 1792 and 1814. He took a personal interest in the park and brought about changes and improvements, including the preservation of game and the commercial production of venison.

Viscount Sidmouth who lived at White Lodge from 1801 to 1844 had a great and lasting influence on the park. Between 1801 and 1816 the 'Hanoverian Hunting Box' was transformed by architect James Wyatt into a self-contained country house surrounded by two hectares of land which was subsequently landscaped by Humphry Repton. In 1831 Sidmouth was appointed deputy ranger and began to transform the old royal hunting ground into a game preserve for hare, grouse and pheasant. During the following 30 years he undertook a systematic programme of establishing plantations almost entirely composed of indigenous forest trees, fenced both to preserve game and to protect the trees from deer. Between 1819 and 1824, Sheen Wood, Sheen Cross Plantation, Spanker's Hill Plantation, Sidmouth Wood and

Breaking through the wall and the many incursions into Richmond Park on enclosure.

Pond Plantation were planted and a nursery for oak trees was established within the park.

The 17 hectare Isabella Plantation was enclosed by Lord Sidmouth in 1831 at which time most of the oak, beech and sweet chestnuts were planted, although some of the oaks are much older. The meaning of 'Isabella' is uncertain and the name may be descriptive rather than referring to a person. Old maps refer to the 'Isabell Slade'. 'Isabell', meaning a dingy yellow, may refer to the colour of the clay topsoil in parts of this garden while a 'slade' is a shallow valley.

At this time other plantations covering half the present park woodland were established. The Terrace Walk of beech from Richmond Gate and the Hornbeam Walk from Pembroke Lodge were planted, and in 1834 Petersham Park was incorporated into Richmond Park. In 1847 Queen Victoria granted Pembroke Lodge to the then Prime Minister, Lord John Russell. During his residence cabinet meetings were held at the lodge and he received many eminent visitors including Queen Victoria herself and the Italian patriot Garibaldi.

Until 1850 no carriages were allowed in the park unless a card of admission from the ranger or his deputy was shown to the gatekeeper. However, from 1886, 'cabs and brakes conveying pleasure parties' could pass through and stop for a picnic. In 1902 the first

bird sanctuary was created at the head of the Upper Pond. The last ranger, Edward VII, took over in 1904 and entrusted the park to the Commissioner of Works. Private shooting was abolished and the preservation of game discontinued when more than 40 hectares of the maturing Sidmouth Plantation was opened to the public, soon to be followed by other plantations. By 1909 the Petersham portion of the park was reserved for school fêtes and bean feasts. On the king's death in 1910 the administration and maintenance passed to the Commissioner of Works, later absorbed by the former Department of the Environment.

During the First World War an army camp was set up and large areas were put under the plough. In the inter-war years the deer herds were restored and the park reverted to a place of public recreation. Again during the Second World War, the war effort took over a large part of the park but all traces of military occupation have long since been removed. After the war a simple stream-side walk was established in the Isabella Plantation. This was the beginning of the woodland garden, further developed between 1951 and 1953 when it was opened to the public.

Catastrophes occurred in 1987 and 1990 when fierce storms destroyed over 1,000 mature trees. To commemorate these two events a new wood was planted called Two Storm Wood. Until the 1950s horses had been the main form of motive power within the royal parks. In 1993 two Shire horses were introduced to Richmond Park whose duties included working in woodland conservation areas, haymaking and litter collection.

Today the park is managed to provide a range of informal grass and woodland regimes. Although some of the grass is mown to provide recreation areas for visitors, the majority is left as grazing meadow for the herds of red deer and dappled fallow deer which wander freely in the park. This grazing has allowed the development of a varied environment rich in wildlife.

Richmond Park is now a site of both national and international importance for wildlife conservation, being designated as a Site of Special Scientific Interest (SSSI), a National Nature Reserve (NNR) and Special Area of Conservation (SAC). These designations primarily relate to the ancient trees and dead wood habitats, the invertebrate assemblage and the areas of acid

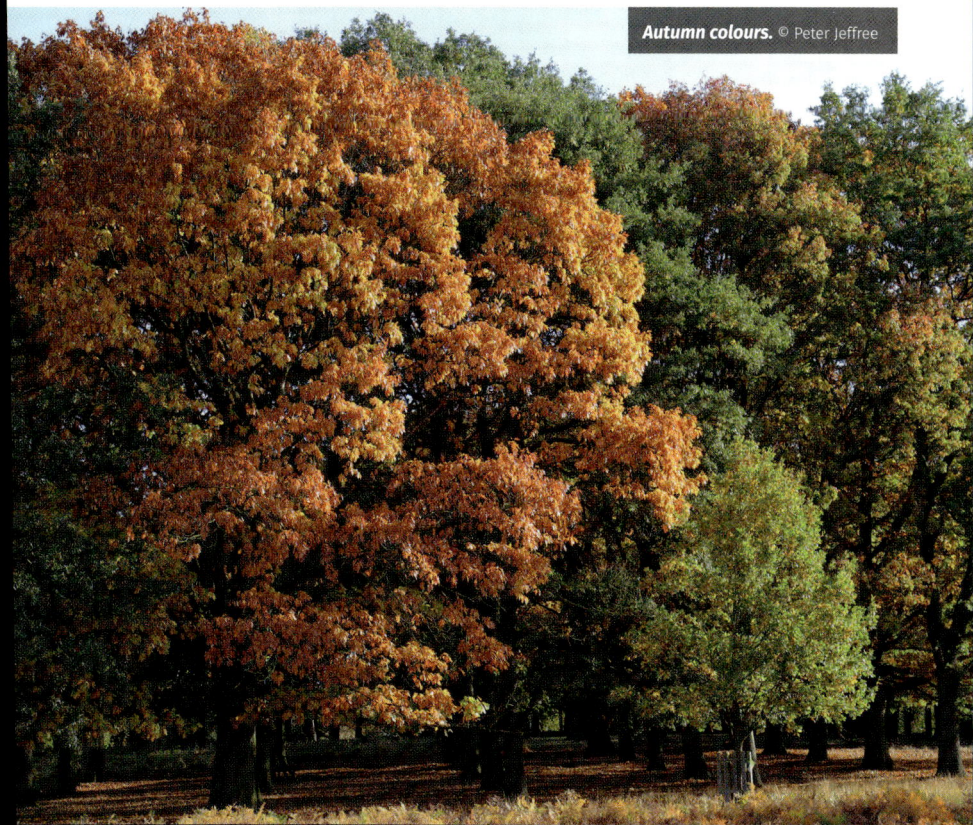

Autumn colours. © Peter Jeffree

grassland. The park was designated as a Site of Special Scientific Interest (SSSI), in 1992. The SSSI designation recognises its diverse deadwood beetle fauna associated with the ancient trees found throughout the parkland.

The park was also designated by English Nature (now Natural England) as a National Nature Reserve (NNR) in 2000 for its habitats and in recognition of its importance as a recreational resource for the London area. Richmond Park is one of the ten largest NNRs in the country, but what makes the park unique is its accessibility. The terrain is very comfortable, and the landscape is appealing to many visitors who can travel here quickly and easily – it is understandably a very popular place to visit. Indeed Richmond Park's 5.5 million visitors per year matches the number of visitors to all 163 NNRs managed directly by Natural England. In addition, the park was also designated as a Special Area of Conservation (SAC) in 2005 due to the population of Stag Beetle *Lucanus cervus* supported on the site. The stag beetle is considered to be globally threatened and is listed as a Species of Principal Importance in the UK Post-2010 Biodiversity Framework.

The Management Plan for the park today states that 'Richmond Park emerges from its historical record as a place whose character is semi-natural, managed, arranged and, to some degree, designed – albeit with a strong response to an expression of nature. The challenge for the future is to maintain the park's essential character, with its managed deer herds, its ancient and successional trees, its extensive open ground and biodiversity balanced with the need to accommodate the reasonable demands and pressures of public access.'

NOT TO BE MISSED ON A VISIT TO RICHMOND PARK

Isabella Plantation

Located in the central southern section of the park, the Isabella Plantation is a fenced woodland area originally enclosed and planted with trees in 1831, with additions and further planting in 1845, 1861, 1865 and 1927. The origins of the 'woodland gardens' can be traced back to initiatives by Joseph Fisher in about 1950 and closely related to similar initiatives at Bushy Park. The gardens were first opened to the public in 1953 and are divided into the publicly accessible and widely visited Woodland Gardens and the non-accessible sanctuary area. Today in excess of 300,000 people visit each year. Isabella Plantation holds a varied and important collection of ornamental trees and shrubs dominated by the genus Rhododendron. Many of the trees and shrubs held are rare. Its internationally important plant collection is similar in quality to other prestigious British woodland gardens including Savill and Valley Gardens at Windsor, Leonardslee, Exbury and Wakehurst Place.

The 'Wilson 50' are a selection of 50 evergreen Kurume azaleas collected by the famous plant hunter Ernest Wilson from Kurume in Japan. He introduced them to America via the Arnold Arboretum in 1919, and then to England. The plantation's Wilson 50 collection was started in 1991. It is now recognised as a National collection by Plant Heritage. The plantation also has a varied and important collection of ornamental trees and shrubs, many of which are rarely seen in public gardens. The plantation also contains in excess of 1,200 Rhododendron which include over 50 different species and about 120 known hybrids, many of which are old hybrids. It also holds a large collection of Camellia which includes many old *Camellia japonica* cultivars, some *Camellia x willliamsii* hybrids as well as an expanding collection of *Camellia sasanqua* varieties.

Isabella Plantation is part of Richmond Park's conservation designation as an SSSI; the site is managed very much with nature in mind and the gardens are run on

A lush and luxuriant Isabella Plantation.

Isabella Plantation in full colour. © Tim Davis

organic principles. Native plants are commonly grown alongside exotics throughout the plantation. The perimeter and shelterbelt areas are planted with native nectar and berry bearing trees and shrubs to provide food and shelter for birds, bats and insects. Ponds and streams are planted with native aquatic and waterside plants. It has year round seasonal colour and successfully blends exotic with native shrubs and trees. Its peak period for colour is between late April and early May when evergreen Kurume azaleas flower with bluebells and emergent foliage alongside the ponds and streams. Recent tree planting has since provided a spectacular display of autumn foliage.

Pond Slade

Pond Slade consists of an open landscape bowl characterised by tussocky wet grassland; drainage channels fall gently north towards Pen Ponds. An almost complete backdrop of woodland hugs the skyline encircling this open bowl, creating a coherent and contained landscape with a sense of tranquillity and serenity. Queen Elizabeth Plantation is located to the northern end of the area. Middle Road runs along its southern edge which is closed to vehicular traffic and provides access to the Isabella Plantation, allowing quiet oversight from passing cyclists, riders and walkers at a distance. A distinctive clump of veteran trees marks the

Pond Slade. © John Saunders

way north towards Pen Ponds. The distinctive glistening stems of the birch trees of the Pen Ponds Plantation gives a hint of the watery landscape beyond.

Pen Ponds

Pen Ponds are a popular destination for visitors to the park. Looking down across the ponds from White Lodge, the valley forms a coherent whole but contains a number of disparate habitats. The man-made ponds have softened over time, with the southern end now a protected enclosure with well-established reed beds backed by a distinctive mixed birch woodland. Elsewhere, some marginal waterside planting, lone willows and a small clump of hawthorn survive. The ponds

Early morning by Pen Ponds. © Bett Atherton

attract a variety of wildfowl and invertebrates whilst skylarks nest on the open slopes below White Lodge. The origin of Upper Pen Pond was probably a smaller pond dug in 1636 by Edward Manning on behalf of Charles I. Lower Pen Pond was probably dug for its gravel as were several other ponds in the park. Both Pen Ponds probably assumed their present form at the end of the seventeenth century, when known as 'The Canals'. The 'Pen' in the name is a reference to a deer pen, of which there were many in the park.

The Queen's Ride

White Lodge was conceived as a hunting lodge for George I. He died in 1727, while it was under construction, and the project was taken over by

George II and Caroline of Ansbach. The Queen's Ride was created in 1736 for Queen Caroline, as part of a series of largely private roads *en route* to Richmond Lodge located on the site of the present Kew Gardens. The framed view down the ride provides an uninterrupted view of White Lodge from the high ground of Sawyers Hill. It is the only accessible visual axis within Richmond Park, making it a unique and unexpected landscape feature (the other, the enclosed Sidmouth Wood/St Paul's vista). The ride creates a formal setting to the lodge and alludes to its historic grandeur as a home for Queen Caroline. The dense mature woodland, which forms the edges of the ride, creates a strong contrast with the open linear nature of the ride. It

White Lodge. © Peter Jeffree

The Queen's Ride.

links Sawpit Plantation to Duchess Wood bisected halfway by the stream leading out of Pen Ponds.

Pembroke Lodge

Pembroke Lodge is found on the site of the Molecatcher's Lodge (also known as the Vermin Killer's Lodge) and appears but is not named on Rocque's Plan of 1774–5. In about 1780, George III granted the lodge 'in the wilderness' to the Countess of Pembroke, and another lodge and stables built towards the present northern entrance of the garden for the gamekeeper Trage who had been the previous occupier of the Molecatcher's Lodge. In 1788 Sir John Soane was asked to make alterations and extensions to the existing cottage and four rooms were added. The southern part of the house is the earliest section and externally this still corresponds closely with Soane's original drawings which show the stepped gable, part of the west elevation. It was constructed of brick and has long been painted white.

The house was again extended between 1792 and 1796 and the kitchen wing added. Both Henry

Holland and Soane were involved in the works. It became known as Pembroke Lodge after the countess's death in 1831. After the death of the countess, at the age of 93, William IV granted the lodge to the Earl of Erroll, husband of one of his daughters. Between 1831 and 1846 the earl completed most of the remainder of the north wing. The Countess of Dunmore lived here during 1846.

In 1847, Queen Victoria granted the lodge to Lord John Russell, then Prime Minister, who conducted much government business there and entertained Queen Victoria, foreign royalty, aristocrats, writers (Dickens, Thackeray, Longfellow, Tennyson) and other notables of the time, including Garibaldi. Lord John was much taken with the lodge – 'an asset that could hardly be equalled, certainly not surpassed in England.' Earl Russell (as he had become) died there on 28 May 1878; Fanny, his second wife, in 1898. Their daughter Lady Agatha Russell left a memorial, still standing in the rose garden: 'Pembroke Lodge 1847–1902. In loving memory of my Father and Mother, Lord and Lady Russell and of our supremely happy home at Pembroke Lodge.' Lord John Russell's grandson, Bertrand Russell, the philosopher and mathematician, grew up there between 1876 and 1894. At Pembroke Lodge, he wrote, 'I grew accustomed to wide horizons and to an unimpeded view of the sunset.'

Georgina, Countess of Dudley took up occupation in 1903 and made further alterations. A wealthy industrialist, John Scott Oliver, took up residence in 1929 and also carried out many alterations, mostly in the north wing. He suffered large financial losses in the recession and put the lodge on the market in 1938. However, before it could be sold, it was requisitioned for services during the Second World War, where the GHQ Liaison Regiment (also known as Phantom) established its regimental headquarters at Pembroke Lodge. Some of the members of the unit went on to become privy councillors, law lords, judges, MPs, a commissioner of the Metropolitan Police (Sir Robert Mark) and actors – including David Niven, who remarked in a letter, 'these were wonderful days which I would not have missed for anything.'

After the Second World War Pembroke Lodge became a government-run tea room with flats for staff. Its conversion to either a restaurant or a country club had been considered earlier in 1926, but it was decided that the income from letting it as a residence would be a better source of revenue. In the early part of the twentieth century, gate-keepers were allowed to serve teas at the gate lodges. The restaurant was opened in 1953 and the flats were occupied by the park staff. In the early 1980s, the upper floor was unused as well as part of the

Pembroke Lodge. © John Johnston

Pembroke Lodge, enjoyed by the thousands who visit every year. © Peter Jeffree

ground floor, and much of the building was damp. Sadly, it seemed Pembroke Lodge was under significant threat as it headed towards the millennium.

To take on the restoration of Pembroke Lodge, Hearsum Family Limited, a private company, entered a partnership with the Royal Parks Agency, in which the company would faithfully restore Pembroke Lodge to its former glory at the company's expense in exchange for the grant of a long-term lease. Some 250,000 people a year now visit the lodge. A huge success and after significant investment, Pembroke Lodge is now unrecognisable from the early 1980s.

Henry VIII's Mound

The site of Henry VIII's Mound was probably a prehistoric burial chamber as ashes were found in it when it was opened in 1835. It was marked on the 1637 plan as 'The King's Standinge', and in a 1683 conveyance document 'King Henry's Mount'. It was later used as a viewpoint for hunting and falconry and is now the viewpoint for a protected vista of St Paul's Cathedral. Henry VIII's Mound has been at the centre of debate over many years and much has already been written 'concerning this earth mound', but it is generally agreed it is a barrow.

Edward Jesse wrote 'This mound has long been celebrated as the spot on which Henry VIII stood to watch the going up of a rocket to assure him that the death of Ann Bolyn [sic] would enable him to marry Lady Jane Seymour. This is the tradition of the park, and it has been handed down from father to son by the several park-keepers.' But this story has been hotly debated for decades and most cast doubt on its authenticity. Anne Boleyn was beheaded on 19 May 1536, and accounts show that on the evening of the same day Henry attended a revel at Wolfe Hall, Wiltshire, some 60 miles away, which would have been a difficult or impossible day's ride for a monarch in those days.

The Mound is on the highest ground in the vicinity, and its first title of 'The King's Standinge' was used in its old sense of a stand for a hunter, to which game would be driven up to be shot. As we know that royalty hunted in the vicinity before the enclosure of the park by Charles I, this seems to be the obvious explanation of the term and the real connection of the tradition with Henry VIII. An interesting feature on many of the old maps, such as John Rocque's map of London, 1741–45 and in Kip's engraving of Petersham Lodge and grounds of about 1720, is the existence of an avenue of trees leading from the Mound in the direction of London, with 'Oliver's Mount' at its termination over 700 yards away. This avenue was evidently replanted about 1830, and can still be plainly seen. When Petersham Park and the Mound were separated from Richmond Park, a high

Henry VIII's Mound. © Peter Jeffree

wooden fence to keep in the deer was in existence between them both. In 1792, a brick ha-ha 171 feet long, 7 feet and 6 inches deep, and 22 feet 8 inches broad, was constructed on the eastern side of the Mound, and that section of the fence was removed to open up a view of London. The rest of the fence was taken away after the re-purchase of Petersham Park, but the ha-ha still remains. During the planting up of Sidmouth Plantation in 1823 it was foreseen that the view would be interfered with. Edward Jesse wrote 'A vista was cut through it, which opens a fine view of London and St Paul's.' This path is still open, and the view open to St Paul's Cathedral from a spot some distance down the path.

Planning restrictions are now in force to ensure the view is not obliterated by tall buildings. These new gates, which can be viewed through the King Henry's Mound telescope, have been installed on the edge of Sidmouth Wood to mark the tercentenary of St Paul's Cathedral. St Paul's remains connected to Richmond Park through the protected ten mile view of the cathedral from King Henry's Mound.

A hidden gem at Richmond Park

The gates, called 'The Way', depict oak branches which morph into a concave top to the gates which suggests a reflection of the cathedral's dome. There is an

The Way. © Peter Jeffree

epigraph of 'The Way' incorporated into the gates and an acknowledgement to Sir Christopher Wren, through a small wren sitting low down in the foliage. A robin sings from the opposite branch. 'The Way' is also an epitaph to Edward Goldsmith, author of the book by the same name.

The bark texture has been created to promote algae and lichen growth low down on the gates to soften the metal work and to ensure it blends with the natural environment of Richmond Park. The gates were kindly donated by the family of renowned environmentalist and *The Ecologist* magazine founder, the late Edward Goldsmith, and were designed by Joshua De Lisle.

INVOLVED WITH RICHMOND PARK

Princess Amelia (1711–1786)

Princess Amelia Sophia Eleonore of Great Britain was the second daughter of King George II of Great Britain and Queen Caroline. Born in Hanover she moved to England when her grandfather, George I, became king. Amelia lived a solitary existence and died in 1786 and was the last surviving child of her parents. As a young woman, Amelia appears to have been somewhat hedonistic and self-centred. The 18 April 1728 edition of the *Post Boy* reported that 'On Saturday, the Princess Amelia set out' [from London] 'for Bath, whither her Highness is to be carry'd in a sedan chair by chairmen, to be relieved in their turns, a coach and six horses attending to carry the chairmen when not on their service.' This journey by the 16-year-old princess commenced on 13 April and ended on 19 April.

In 1751, Princess Amelia became ranger of Richmond Park after the death of Robert Walpole, Second Earl of Orford. Immediately afterwards, the princess caused major public uproar by closing the park to the public, only allowing a few close friends and those with special permits to enter. This continued until 1758 when John Lewis took the gatekeeper, who stopped him from entering the park, to court. The court ruled in favour of Lewis, citing the fact that, when Charles I enclosed the park in the seventeenth century, he allowed the public right of way in the park. Princess Amelia was forced to lift the restrictions.

Despite her attempts at Richmond Park, the princess was generous in her gifts to charitable organisations. In 1760 she donated £100 to the society for educating poor orphans of clergymen (later the Clergy Orphan Corporation) to help pay for a school for twenty-one orphan daughters of clergymen of the Church of England. In 1783 she agreed to become an annual subscriber of £25 to the new County Infirmary in Northampton.

In 1761, Princess Amelia became the owner of Gunnersbury Estate, Middlesex, purchased from the estate of Henry Furnese. Princess Amelia used Gunnersbury as her summer residence. She added a chapel and at some time between 1777 and 1784, she commissioned a bath house, extended as a folly by a subsequent owner of the land in the nineteenth century, which still stands today and is known as Princess Amelia's Bathhouse. She also owned a property in Cavendish Square, Soho, London, where she died unmarried on 31 October 1786, at which time she was the last surviving child of King George II and Queen Caroline.

Princess Amelia Sophia Eleonore of Great Britain, 1745. © Yale Center for British Art, Paul Mellon Collection

A miniature of her first cousin, Frederick of Prussia, was found on her body. The great king originally intended for her had died two months earlier. She was buried in the Henry VII Lady Chapel in Westminster Abbey.

John Lewis (1713–1792)

John Lewis was a Richmond resident who owned a brewery near the Thames close to where Terrace Gardens now are. Lewis became a local celebrity after his battles with Princess Amelia. His portrait was painted by T. Stewart, a pupil of Sir Joshua Reynolds, and the picture currently hangs in the reference library at the Old Town Hall, Richmond. An engraving was later made by Robert Field, a copy of which was said in the eighteenth century to hang in many homes in the area. On the engraving were the words of Rev. Thomas Wakefield: 'Be it remembered that by the steady perseverance of John Lewis, brewer, at Richmond, Surry' [sic] 'the right of a free passage through Richmond Park was recovered and established by the laws of his country (notwithstanding very strongly opposed) after being upwards of twenty years withheld from the people.'

The court case had been a heavy financial burden on Lewis. His brewery was also flooded, and his means of livelihood was gone. Thomas Wakefield organised a collection for Lewis, and this resulted in a small annuity on which Lewis survived for some years. A further effort to secure money for him was being made at the time of his death in 1792. He was buried at

Portrait of Brewer, John Lewis, by T. Stewart from 1758. By permission of the London Borough of Richmond upon Thames Borough Art Collection, Orleans House Gallery

Remembered in the park today.

St Mary Magdalene, the parish church of Richmond. The horizontal gravestone can be seen outside the church's South side. The inscription reads: 'Here lie the remains of Mr John Lewis, Late of this parish who died, The 22 of October 1792, Aged 79 years'.

Henry Addington, 1st Viscount Sidmouth (1757–1844)

Henry Addington, 1st Viscount Sidmouth, PC was a British Tory statesman who served as Prime Minister of the United Kingdom from 1801 to 1804. Addington is best known for obtaining the Treaty of Amiens in 1802, an unfavourable peace with Napoleonic France which marked the end of the Second Coalition during the French Revolutionary Wars. When that treaty broke down he resumed the war, but he was without allies and conducted relatively weak defensive hostilities, ahead of what would become the War of the Third Coalition. He was forced from office in favour of William Pitt the Younger, who had preceded Addington as Prime Minister. Addington is also known for his reactionary crackdown on advocates of democratic reforms during a 10-year spell as Home Secretary from 1812 to 1822. He is the longest continuously serving holder of that office since it was created in 1782.

In 1801 King George III decided that Henry Addington, his new Prime

Henry Addington, later first Viscount Sidmouth, 1785 to 1786. © Yale Center for British Art, Paul Mellon Collection

Minister, should have a suitable house near the capital, and gave him White Lodge. The king ordered extensive works of improvement to White Lodge, including the building up of the quadrant corridors. Addington remained in occupation after giving up the premiership (when he was created Viscount Sidmouth), and in 1813 he was appointed deputy ranger, a post which he held until his death in 1844. He carried out a major programme of new plantations, including one which still bears his name.

Bertrand Russell (1872–1970)

Bertrand Arthur William Russell was an influential British logician, philosopher, and mathematician, working mostly in the twentieth century. A Nobel prize-winner, Russell was a significant figure in the history of philosophy and politics who spent most of his childhood at Pembroke Lodge here in Richmond Park. Bertrand, who became the 3rd Earl Russell, was born into one of Britain's leading Whig families. His paternal grandfather, Lord John Russell, was Prime Minister in the 1840s and 1860s, and had been granted use of Pembroke Lodge as a residence by Queen Victoria. Following the death of both his parents, at the age of four young Bertrand came to live at the Lodge, to be brought up by his grandparents. Bertrand recalls in his autobiography that when he arrived in 1876 he was 'placed upon the high stool for tea.'

A prolific writer, Bertrand Russell was also a populariser of philosophy and a commentator on a large variety of topics, ranging from very serious issues to the mundane. Continuing a family tradition in political affairs, he was a prominent liberal as well as a socialist and anti-war activist for most of his long life. Millions looked up to Russell as a prophet of the creative and rational life; at the same time, his stances on many topics were extremely controversial.

Born at the height of Britain's economic and political ascendancy, he died of influenza nearly a century later when the British Empire had all but vanished. As one of the world's best-known intellectuals, Russell's voice carried enormous moral authority, even into his early nineties. Among his other political activities, Russell was a vigorous proponent of nuclear disarmament and an outspoken critic of the American war in Vietnam. In 1950, Russell was made a Nobel Laureate in Literature 'in recognition of his varied and significant writings in which he champions humanitarian ideals and freedom of thought.'

Bertrand Russell in 1949.

7

HYDE PARK
A PARK FOR THE PEOPLE

Our friend Richard Church is a little less effusive about Hyde Park in his 1956 introduction to it, preferring to almost immediately compare and contrast the park with Kensington Gardens. 'Indistinguishably joined, the two parks are different in character, though it is not easy to define that difference. But Speaker's Corner, at the extreme north-east corner of Hyde Park, needs only to be contrasted with the Sunken Garden in the precincts of Kensington Palace at the farther end of Kensington Gardens, for the contrast to be appreciated. The two spots are two miles apart. They are also two centuries apart.' Indeed they are, and absolutely, they are both very different. However, there has been more public access to Hyde Park throughout its history than any other royal park, and this has impacted on its character today.

Two Roman roads crossed at what is now the north-eastern corner of Hyde Park: Watling Street (now the Edgware Road) from north to south and the *Via Trinobantina* (now Oxford Street and the Bayswater Road) from east to west.

These two roads largely determined the boundaries of the park.

In medieval times the largest gallows in London – the notorious Tyburn 'tree' – was located at the crossroads outside the park. The gallows, built to a triangular plan, could hang eight men on each of three sides. Although it survived until 1783, the precise location is unknown. However, there is a commemorative stone on the ground near Marble Arch, a reminder of the many highwaymen, thieves and dissenting priests who met their end here over the centuries.

Hyde Park is first recorded as forming part of the Manor of Eia, the official estate of the Master of the Horse. 'Eia' meant 'island' to the Saxons, for through the land ran the Westbourne stream, a tributary of the Thames, and the Tyburn stream, from which the gallows took its name. The Domesday Book records that the manor was split into three, one being the Manor of Hyde. ('Hyde' probably referred to deer hyde or hide.) Geoffrey de Mandeville had acquired it as a reward for his services at the Battle of Hastings, and in his will he passed it on to the Benedictine monks of St Peter, Westminster. The monks cleared some of the forest and started to cultivate the land. It became a royal park in 1536 when the site, which was excellent for hunting, inhabited as it was by deer and wild boar, caught the eye of Henry VIII. He compelled the abbot to agree to an exchange of land.

Another tradition was established in Tudor times when Elizabeth I reviewed her troops in the park. The Parade Ground, the wide open space parallel to Park Lane, takes its name from this kind of military use. However for the most part, the park remained a private hunting ground for nearly a century, until James I came to the throne. He permitted limited access and it became a centre of fashion and pleasure. A ranger, or keeper, was appointed by the king to take charge of the park, together with a pond keeper responsible for the string of ten ponds. A large enclosure called The Ring provided a circular drive where courtiers and their families drove round daily in lavish equipages. This was an amazing spectacle for all to see and is captured in many illustrations of the time.

In 1637 the park was opened to the public by Charles I (the same year that Richmond Park was finally enclosed as a new hunting ground). But under Oliver Cromwell's Roundhead parliament, its use for fashionable display ceased and a large square

The Action between the British & American Frigates on the Serpentine, Hyde Park 1 August 1814. © Yale Center for British Art, Paul Mellon Collection

fort with four bastions was built in the south-east of the park. At the restoration of the monarchy the park was quickly handed back to Charles II. He opened it all, and replaced the wooden fence with a brick wall.

In 1665, the year of the Great Plague, many citizens of London fled the city

and Westminster to camp on Hyde Park's great open spaces. Soldiers stationed in the capital to keep order as the disease ravaged the population were also encamped in the park.

Towards the end of the seventeenth century, in the reign of William III and Mary II, the court was established at Kensington Palace, partly due to William's poor health and the need for the fresh air at Kensington. As the park had become notorious for footpads and thieves, the king had the road between St James's and his palace lit with 300 oil lamps. This, the first artificially lit highway in the country, became the New Carriage Road or 'Route de Roi' – Rotten Row. However, people who wanted to go through the park at night continued to wait until sufficient numbers had collected, then travelled together for mutual protection.

During the eighteenth century, George II's wife, Queen Caroline, had the then royal gardener John Bridgeman carry out extensive renovations to the landscape. Primarily these involved the creation of a sinuous lake which became known as the Serpentine of Hyde Park and the Long Water of Kensington Gardens.

Hyde Park became a venue for national celebrations. In 1814 the Prince Regent organised a fair, festivities and fireworks to mark the end of the Napoleonic Wars. The climax was a re-enactment on the Serpentine of one of Lord Nelson's naval battles. On another occasion, this time to honour his accession to the throne as George IV, elephants were towed on rafts on the Serpentine.

Later in the nineteenth century, during the reign of Queen Victoria, West Carriage Drive was created and in 1851 The Great Exhibition was held in the park. This spectacular celebration of art and inventive genius was housed in the specially erected Crystal Palace designed by Sir Joseph Paxton. The building, covering almost 8 hectares, was located between South Carriage Drive and Rotten Row in line with Prince of Wales Gate. Victoria visited the Crystal Palace frequently until it was removed at the end of the exhibition.

The Crystal Palace in Hyde Park, 1852.
© Yale Center for British Art, Paul Mellon Collection

Winter Wonderland in Hyde Park. © John Pavel

Public speaking in the park has become an important tradition, first recorded in 1855. In 1866 Edmund Beales' 'Reform League' challenged the decision that the park could not be used for demonstrations and public speaking by holding an unauthorised meeting. Railings were pulled out and plants destroyed. In 1867 two further meetings were held with no trouble and the right of assembly was established in 1872.

During the Second World War there were gun emplacements in the park. Air-raid shelters were built and allotments provided fresh vegetables in the 'Dig for Victory' campaign. Improvements to the park over time have been considerable with the completion of the Dorchester Ride in 1990 and the opening of the Queen Elizabeth Gate in 1993, and into the twenty-first century, improvements to Speaker's Corner and the provision of refreshments in the park.

Historically Hyde Park is divided from Kensington Gardens along a line which runs from Alexandra Gate in the south, over the Serpentine Bridge, up Buck Hill Walk to Victoria Gate on the Bayswater Road. Nowadays the West Carriage Drive marks the boundary for all practical purposes. Today it is the host to some of the largest events in the city – from Winter Wonderland to summertime festivals.

The impact of Decimus Burton, Wellington Arch and Hyde Park Corner

The finest entrance to Hyde Park is Apsley Gate, an elegant Greek Revival screen with an adjacent lodge, both by architect Decimus Burton when he was only 25 years old. Burton was the tenth child of James Burton who was a London builder who developed large areas of Bloomsbury and the houses around Regent's Park. Decimus Burton's works in London were considerable and included the gate or screen here at Hyde Park Corner; the Wellington Arch, and gates; Green Park and St James's Park; Regent's Park (including Cornwall Terrace, York Terrace, Clarence Terrace, Chester Terrace, and the villas of the

Decimus Burton.

Inner Circle which included his own mansion, The Holme); the enclosure of the forecourt of Buckingham Palace from which he had Nash's Marble Arch moved; the clubhouse of the Athenaeum Club, London; Carlton House Terrace; Spring Gardens in St James's; and the Palm House and the Temperate House at Kew Gardens.

Burton's most impressive addition to Hyde Park though is his Greek Revival screen. It was made from Portland stone and built between 1826–29. It combines a triumphal arch with an Ionic colonnade and the frieze by John Henning is copied directly from the Elgin Marbles that were originally on the Parthenon in Athens. Alongside his work in Hyde Park, Burton also designed a new western approach to Buckingham Palace. Apsley Gate was planned as the final part of a route that would run from Nash's Marble Arch, which originally stood in front of the palace, through his own Constitution Arch into Hyde Park.

Also on Hyde Park Corner, is the Wellington Arch, also designed by Decimus Burton and commissioned in the 1820s as a commemoration of Britain's victory against the French in the Napoleonic Wars. However, it never quite achieved its designer's full vision. As the money ran out, much of the planned ornamentation never happened, including a symbolic sculpture with a four-horse chariot or

The Grand Entrance to Hyde Park, 1844. © Yale Center for British Art, Paul Mellon Collection

Hyde Park Corner and Decimus Burton's magnificent entrance. © Peter Jeffree

The Wellington Arch. © Peter Jeffree

quadriga on top. It was finished in 1830 and originally stood opposite Burton's Hyde Park screen, and served both as an entrance to Green Park and a grand outer entrance to Buckingham Palace.

In 1838, it was decided that there should be a national memorial to the Duke of Wellington, and that it should stand on top of what was then called the Green Park Arch. Matthew Cotes Wyatt was invited to produce an equestrian statue which he took six years to make and caused, again, much controversy. The arch had to be strengthened to take the sculpture and the eventual 40-ton statue was lifted

into position in 1846, and was subject to much derision. Described by many as a 'monstrosity', it was totally out of proportion to the arch and was even debated in parliament. Yet, despite its unpopularity, it remained there for many years. With increasing traffic in the area in the 1880s, a new road system was devised and the arch was dismantled and moved to its present position without the statue, which is now near the army camp in Aldershot. The current statue which resides on top of the arch was designed by Adrian Jones and was favoured by the Prince of Wales, having seen a plaster of a sculpture called *Triumph* by Jones in 1891 at the Royal Academy. Eventually funded by Lord Michelham, it was erected in 1912 with no official unveiling. Known as the Quadriga, it represents a boy driving four horses with the winged figure of 'Peace' alighting in the chariot they are pulling.

The Statue of Achilles

Nearby Apsley House was the home of the Duke of Wellington, whose statue by Richard Westmacott stands nearby. The 18-foot statue of Achilles, the Greek hero of the Trojan War, commemorates the soldier and politician, Arthur Wellesley, 1st Duke of Wellington (1769–1852). It was installed by order of King George III and unveiled on 18 June 1822. It was Hyde Park's first statue and was its most controversial. Loosely described as Achilles, the huge figure was cast in bronze obtained from cannons captured in Wellington's campaigns. The image was taken from a Roman group on Monte Cavallo but its head was clearly modelled on the duke

Achilles, a tribute to the Duke of Wellington. © Peter Jeffree

himself. What was controversial was that the statue was also nude and this did not go down very well. The Ladies of England, who had commissioned it, were horrified, the press delighted and the offensive member ultimately covered by a small fig leaf. Achilles is one of five commemorations of the 'Iron Duke'.

The Dell Restaurant

The canopied Dell restaurant was built in 1965 and was designed by architect Patrick Gwynne. It is one of the few modern buildings in the Royal Parks of any worthy architectural merit. It replaced the Ring Tea House and was redeveloped again in 1979.

Gwynne (1913–2003) was a British modernist architect with Welsh roots. As an architect, Gwynne specialised in houses. His designs have a 'collective resemblance in their ingenious adaptation to site and prospect, their logical but often dramatic internal planning, and their willingness to use curved forms on plan'. Gwynne also grew a significant reputation for restaurant design. His entry in the restaurant competition at the Festival of Britain led to a commission for the Crescent Restaurant in nearby Battersea Park. Through this he met Charles Forte, for whom he went on in 1964 to design the Serpentine Restaurant in Hyde Park, a series of mushroom structures inspired

The Serpentine Restaurant, overlooking the Serpentine lake. © Peter Jeffree

by umbrellas – which he thought appropriate in a park. It was demolished in 1990, but his smaller Dell Restaurant, built in 1965, at the other end of the park survives, and the terrazzo terrace and built-in seating overlooking the Serpentine show his signature touches.

Lansbury's Lido

During the General Strike of 1926 Hyde Park was used as a food depot for London, and closed to the public. In the spring of 1930 Hyde Park took on yet another phase. For 200 years, there had been no swimming in the Serpentine, except in the early mornings, and even then, only men and boys had been allowed to swim. But Mr George Lansbury had become First Commissioner of Works, with authority over all the public parks. Lansbury's public spirit was well known and it was not long before he set out to make Hyde Park a more cheerful place for young and old, men and women alike. Through his office, bathing establishments were erected on the Serpentine, which came to be known as 'Lansbury's Lido'. Older people had never needed any encouragement to bathe in the Serpentine, having always been well represented in the traditional early morning swim. Lansbury's innovation was twofold: it enabled Londoners to bathe at all times of the day, and

The Lido Pavilion and Restaurant. © Gary Knight

The Lido, popular with summer bathers.

opened the Serpentine for the first time for 200 years, since it had been founded, to women. Since then it has become incredibly popular with thousands bathing there annually. Naturally, some opposition occurred, including a woman doctor in 1932 who pleaded that she did not see any need for people to wear costumes in the Serpentine as Hyde Park was Nature's Park. Questions were also asked in parliament as to whether the Serpentine was a fit place to bathe and whether there was not pollution caused by streptococci with so many people about in the water. The new Lido pavilion was eventually erected with the assistance of £5,000 donated by a Mr D'Arcy Cooper in memory of his son. It was reconstructed in 1951–2.

The Joy of Life Fountain

Adjacent to Park Lane is the Joy of Life fountain, which is a joy to behold. It dates from 1963 when Park Lane was widened, and donated by the Constance Fund with its gravity-defying bronze figures sculpted by T.B. Huxley-Jones and cast at the Peckham Foundry. The fountain depicts two bronze figures holding hands

The Joy of Life Fountain. © Peter Jeffree

while appearing to dance above the water, with four bronze children emerging from the pool. It replaced the Boy and Dolphin Fountain which previously stood on this spot and was felt to be out of place with the new Park Lane boulevard scheme. Over 100 years ago, this part of Hyde Park was once a much-admired Victorian sunken garden created in the 1860s. However, long before that it was a reservoir supplying the royal palaces with drinking water.

The Diana, Princess of Wales Fountain

The Diana, Princess of Wales (1961–1997) memorial fountain is a memorial dedicated to the 'People's Princess'.

It was designed to express Diana's spirit and love of children and was opened in July 2004. Diana was seen as a contemporary and accessible princess, so the goal of the memorial fountain was to allow people to access the structure and the water for quiet wading and contemplation. The design aimed to reflect Diana's life, with water flowing from the highest point in two directions as it cascades, swirls and bubbles before meeting in a calm pool at the bottom. It contains 545 pieces of Cornish granite – each shaped by the latest computer-controlled machinery and pieced together using traditional skills. The water is constantly being refreshed and is drawn from London's water table. The memorial

The Diana, Princess of Wales Fountain. © Peter Jeffree

also symbolises Diana's quality and openness with three bridges where the water can be crossed leading to the heart of the fountain.

Speakers' Corner

Speakers' Corner is located on the north-east edge of Hyde Park, nearest Marble Arch and Oxford Street. Historic figures such as Karl Marx, Vladimir Lenin and George Orwell were known to often use the area to demonstrate free speech. In 1872, an Act of Parliament set aside this part of Hyde Park for public speaking. Even today, on a Sunday morning, it's not unusual to find crowds gathering at Speakers' Corner to listen to enthusiasts expounding their views. Anyone can turn up unannounced to speak on any subject, as long as the police consider their speeches lawful.

Close to this spot, about 250 years ago, people were still being hanged at the infamous Tyburn gallows. The gallows were installed in 1196 and by the time they were dismantled in 1783 more than 50,000 people had been executed here. Everyone condemned to die at Tyburn could make a final speech. Some confessed whereas others protested their innocence or criticised the authorities. For onlookers, executions at Tyburn were big social events. Londoners could buy a ticket to watch executions from a seat on huge wooden platforms. Eventually, the authorities decided the hangings

were too rowdy and transferred them to Newgate Prison. But the tradition of protest and pleasure in Hyde Park continued.

The origins of Speakers' Corner as it is known today stem from 1866, when a meeting of the Reform League demanding the extension of the franchise was suppressed by the government. Marches and protests had long convened or terminated their routes in Hyde Park, often at Speakers' Corner itself. Finding the park locked, demonstrators tore up hundreds of yards of railings to gain access, and three days of rioting followed. The next year, when a crowd of 150,000 defied another government ban and marched to Hyde Park, police and troops did not intervene. Spencer Walpole, the Home Secretary, resigned the next day. In the 1872 Parks Regulation Act, the right to meet and speak freely in Hyde Park was established through a series of regulations governing the conduct of meetings. The speaking area of Hyde Park as defined in legislation extends far beyond Speakers' Corner but it is here where most people congregate. In addition, Hyde Park's long tradition of accommodating large public demonstrations and rallies continues today.

From 1906 to 1914 the suffragettes held large and small meetings in Hyde Park as part of their campaign for votes for women. In the summer of 1906 they had a meeting every week near to the Reformer's tree. During the Women's Day of 21 June 1908, 250,000 women marched to Hyde Park to hear 20 different speaking platforms. In 1913 the police banned the Women's Social and Political Union from meeting in the park, but the suffragettes defiantly continued to do so.

By the 1930s 'soapbox' orators were to be found in marketplaces, street corners and parks across the country. Of the estimated one hundred speaking places found weekly in London between 1855 and 1939, Speakers' Corner is the last to survive.

Speakers' Corner was the focus of a huge rally in February 2003 against military action in Iraq. The number of people who attended was estimated at between 750,000 and two million. The speakers and supporters included the actress Vanessa Redgrave, human rights campaigner Bianca Jagger, former MP Tony Benn, playwright Harold Pinter and the Hollywood actor, Tim Robbins. This rally was one of the most recent in Hyde Park about war. In 1859, there were demonstrations about the Franco–Austrian War. Since an Act of Parliament in 1872, Speakers'

Speakers' Corner – and passion resonates.

Speakers' Corner – religious debate dominates today.

Corner has provided a focus for people to express their views about a range of topics from voting rights, the price of bread, to Sunday trading. It is a remarkable space.

A hidden gem at Hyde Park – Memorial to W.H. Hudson

Another controversial introduction to Hyde Park was in 1925 with the introduction of a memorial to the writer and naturalist W.H. Hudson, who had studied the birds in the Royal Parks. He also helped to establish the Royal Society for the Protection of Birds and campaigned for wild areas in parks, at a time when they were always neat and tidy.

Located in the bird sanctuary to the south of the Frame Ground, it could easily be missed today but is a fitting tribute to one of our greatest naturalists. It did take some considerable time though before it was considered acceptable. The journalist H.J. Massingham reckoned, 'the large eagle-like bird in the sculpture must be a portrait statue of old Hudson himself. When I used to ... lunch with him at Whiteley's, it was like taking one of the hunched eagles at the zoo out of his cage for an airing.' At its unveiling,

The Hudson Memorial. © Peter Jeffree

there was, however, uproar when the memorial was unveiled by Stanley Baldwin in 1925. Not only were the sides of the pool too steep to allow birds to drink or bathe, the real perceived horror lay in Jacob Epstein's relief carving of *Rima*, Hudson's spirit of the forest, the child goddess of nature who featured in Hudson's novel *Green Mansions*, published in 1904. *The Daily Mail* was no fan. 'Take this horror out of the park!'. Many dignitaries of the day signed a letter to the *Morning Post* which said: 'It would be a reproach to all concerned if future generations were allowed to imagine that this piece of artistic anarchy in any way reflects the spirit of the age.' It did, though, have its supporters and sense eventually prevailed. George Bernard Shaw, Sybil Thorndike and Augustus John lent their names to a letter in *The Times* and artist Muirhead Bone argued their case with the Commissioner of Works. Ironically, it is now considered one of Epstein's finest early works.

INVOLVED WITH HYDE PARK

George Lansbury (1859–1940)

George Lansbury was a lifelong socialist and supporter of women's rights, along with his wife, daughters, sons and daughters-in-law. Speaking in the House of Commons on 22 May 1912, Lansbury stated, 'There are working women... No one will want to argue that these women have undertaken this imprisonment, and the torture of forcible feeding merely for the fun of the thing or merely to get notoriety.'

On entering the Commons in 1910, Lansbury quickly affirmed his support for women's suffrage and for women campaigners, however militant their actions. However, in November 1912, frustrated by the Labour Party's position on the issue, he decided to resign his seat and seek re-election as a women's suffrage candidate.

Lansbury's campaign was enthusiastically supported by all the major women's suffrage societies.

George Lansbury and the opening of Lansbury's Lido.

However, in the wider Labour Party and the press, attitudes were divided and often hostile. His behaviour was described as 'quixotic'. The by-election resulted in a narrow victory for the Unionist (Conservative) Party. Lansbury did not regain the seat until 1922 and served until his death in 1940. Lansbury continued to support the women's cause after his defeat in 1912. He defended escalating suffragette militancy and criticised the treatment of suffrage prisoners under the 'Cat and Mouse' Act. In 1913, Lansbury was accused of 'inciting to crime' and imprisoned. He went on hunger strike but, after vehement complaints from MPs, was quickly released, ironically, under the conditions of the Act he had so passionately condemned. He stated 'I believe that this fight for women's enfranchisement is the biggest fight socially that is going on in our country.'

Newsreel scenes from 1930 show sun-worshipping Londoners testing the waters at the newly opened Hyde Park lido. The happily-timed heatwave of August 1930 hit Britain during the height of a bathing-craze. The freshly-opened Hyde Park lido was the initiative of Commissioner of Works and popular socialist figure George Lansbury, who pushed for improved public recreation facilities. Unofficially known as 'Lansbury's Lido', it allowed for mixed bathing and sunbathing on the Serpentine for the first time, and remains a popular London oasis today.

8

REGENT'S PARK
A ROYAL PARTNERSHIP

The amount of visitors to the Royal Parks today numbers in excess of 77 million, with Hyde Park experiencing nearly 13 million, St James's Park just under 17 million, Kensington Gardens over 10 million and Regent's Park 8 million. Whilst visits to many of them may seem busy, there is certainly solitude to be found in each of them. Richard Church, writing in 1956 is 'impressed by the quietness of Regent's Park' and suggests that this 'may account for the wide variety of bird life to be found there.'

In common with other Royal Parks, the area covered by Regent's Park formed part of the vast chase appropriated by Henry VIII. This wide tract of wooded pasture was known as Marylebone Park Fields, after the parish church of Tybourne Village dedicated to St Mary at the Bourne. This name is a reminder that Regent's Park is well watered, though the Tyburn which crossed its boundaries on its course to the River Thames is no longer visible. As a hunting ground the only boundaries were a ditch and rampart, and the park was an invigorating ride from the Palace of Whitehall. Marylebone Park, as it was known, remained a royal chase until 1646, when Charles I mortgaged it to two of his supporters during the Civil War to pay for arms.

During Oliver Cromwell's interregnum, the land was sold and stripped of trees to pay debts, and 3,000 trees were reserved for naval construction. With the restoration of the monarchy in 1600 the park returned to the crown and was let as pasture to a number of tenant farmers. By the end of the eighteenth century, terraced streets and squares were appearing and becoming fashionable south of the New Road (now Marylebone Road). The crown (through the Commissioners of Woods and Forests) became aware of the area's potential and decided not to renew the leases which were due to end in 1811. A design competition was held and a number of schemes drawn up. It was John Nash, the newly appointed architect to the crown and friend of the Prince Regent, who finally drew together the ideas into an ambitious development which would transform the heart of London. Instead of simply extending the city on the usual grid pattern with open squares, a vast rounded park would be created, surrounded by palatial terraces and containing a lake and canal, fifty six villas and, somewhat apart, a second home or retreat for the prince. Also part of the scheme was a major new processional route from the Prince Regent's main residence at Carlton House (on the northern edge of St James's Park), via newly completed buildings in Portland Place, to a new circus which would mark the grand entrance to Regent's Park. However, the development changed during the course of construction, and the prince's attention was diverted to other projects. In Regent's Park the proposed royal retreat was never built and the number of villas was reduced to eight.

The proposed circus entrance from Portland Place was modified to form Park Crescent and Park Square, and the canal (now Regent's Canal) was moved to the northern boundary of the park. Despite these changes, the original framework has allowed the development of the park into areas of differing character which fit successfully in the overall design. Initially Regent's Park was not open to the public and access was restricted to people living in the surrounding properties and to those with carriages, who could drive north from Mayfair to enjoy the perimeter drive.

The Holme, one of the few remaining villas in Regent's Park. © Peter Jeffree

The Zoological Gardens in Regent's Park. © Yale Center for British Art, Paul Mellon Collection

The park became the home for several learned societies. The new Zoological Society of London was first to move in. Its architect was none other than Decimus Burton and the gardens won a place on the carriage circuit for a number of years. The vision of the zoological gardens in which buildings would be ornaments persisted for many years to come. In 1839 the Royal Botanic Society took over the land within the Inner Circle and created a central lawn, a lake and associated mound, conservatory (again designed by Decimus Burton), and a number of gardens for special groups of plants including American, medicinal, herbaceous and agricultural, together with a museum and nursery. Access was restricted to members and their friends.

A third society – the Toxophilite – introduced archery and also provided additional sport in winter when it flooded its land for the London Skating Club. This mixture of gardens and open air activities has continued to this day.

In London, building developments were steadily encroaching on the surrounding fields. Parliament was concerned about the need to provide open-air recreation for the poorer people as well as the wealthy. As a result the east side of the park was opened in 1835, followed by the north-west grasslands in 1841 (when Primrose Hill was added). At the time, this was reported in *The Times* as an initiative aimed at 'redemption of the working class through recreation, after all why

The former hot-house in the Royal Botanic Gardens, designed by Decimus Burton.

should the lower orders not enjoy the liberty of taking a walk in the more plebeian portions of the park... provided they have a decent coat on'. In 1845 the general public was admitted to the park on two days of the week and, for a small payment, allowed entrance to the zoo.

Prince Albert presided over the creation of the formal gardens at the southern end of the Broad Walk, the site of today's Avenue Gardens. This was one of the first areas to be opened to the public in 1835. The prince expressly requested that William Andrews Nesfield should be employed to redesign this area and his plans for a flower garden were implemented in 1864. The new layout was flanked by the outer rows

of existing Wych Elms and by the inner row of Horse Chestnuts along the Broad Walk. Victorian bedding schemes were then at their most complex and the gardens, also known as the Italian Gardens, were highly ornate with ornamental tazzas and vases for plants (some of these which still remain), gravel paths and railings.

Queen Mary's Gardens, named after the consort of George V, date back to the early 1930s, when the Royal Botanic Society decided that it could not afford to renew its lease on the area within the Inner Circle. The area was redesigned as part of the park with new gardens, an open air theatre and café. The new name also confirmed the royal connection.

Within the northern boundary of the park a golf and tennis school was established. A number of the remaining villas changed from being private houses to becoming public institutions.

During the Second World War the park was taken over by the military for encampments and to house personnel. More than 300 bombs, including incendiaries and V2 rockets, fell in the park, causing great devastation. Land that was once undulating is now flat because the park was used to dump bomb rubble, which is almost

The Broad Walk in Regent's Park – relaxing, reading the latest news, feet resting on a foot plate.

three metres deep in places. There was also considerable debate about the future of Nash's Regency terraces after the war, with many damaged almost beyond repair from air raids. The Gorrell Commission set up in 1946 thankfully concluded that the terraces should be restored and ignored the advice of the Marylebone Labour Party who called for their demolition and replacement with social housing.

Today, Regent's Park and the surrounding terraces, with every lamp post, bollard, railing or gate pier, is protected. Regent's Park is, as Nash wrote in 1813, 'one entire Park compleat in unity of character.'

We should not ignore the adjacent Primrose Hill. Like Regent's Park, this area was once part of a great chase, appropriated by Henry VIII. In the twelfth century it was described as being 'full of the lairs and coverts of beasts and game, stags, bucks, boars and wild bulls,' and as late as 1778 it was approached 'by way of deep and dirty lanes'. Primrose Hill, with its clear rounded skyline, was purchased from Eton College in 1841 to extend the parkland available to the poor people of northern London for open-air recreation. It has over many years had a 'lively reputation' where duels were fought and prize-fights took place, with Mother Shipton making threatening prophesies about what would happen if the city sprawl was allowed to encroach on its boundaries: 'When London surrounds Primrose Hill the streets of the Metropolis will run with blood.'

Today, Primrose Hill has a number of facilities including an outdoor gymnasium which has been present since Victorian times and a network of paths which criss-cross the hill. The top of the hill today provides one of the finest views in London, a view now protected through planning legislation.

NOT TO BE MISSED ON A VISIT TO REGENT'S PARK AND PRIMROSE HILL

Regent's Park Terraces

Regent's Park Terraces are London's finest example of scenic architecture. They define the space that is Regent's Park. John Nash designed the full elevations for the buildings enclosing the park and was then involved with the detailed design of: Cumberland Terrace, Chester Terrace, Cambridge Terrace, York Terrace, Sussex Place, Hanover Terrace and Kent Terrace. Cumberland Terrace is the most palatial of them all, yet behind the Corinthian columns, crowning pediments and triumphal arches, are rows of identical terraces. The nearby terrace of Gloucester Gate, for instance, was the subject of Nash's famous remark that the parts looked larger than he expected. His designs

Above: *Cumberland Terrace, one of Nash's finest achievements.* © Peter Jeffree

Below: *Sussex Place.* © Peter Jeffree

were worked up by draughtsmen (including a young Decimus Burton) from the briefest of sketches and carried out, with considerable licence, by speculating builders.

The Avenue Gardens

The Avenue Gardens were originally planted by Nash as the Broad Walk with eight rows of trees, but many of them did not thrive and were the subject of many inspections and reports. In the end, it was down to landscape architect William Andrews Nesfield who put forward a design for new formal gardens. This required the removal of the inner rows of stunted trees. The strongly geometric layout of 1863 included extravagant bedding schemes and imposing tazzas. With their original Nesfield design severely compromised, they were restored in the 1990s with many new fountains and tazzas copied from the nineteenth-century catalogues of Austin and Seeley (a Marylebone firm) that Nesfield had at his disposal. The only original is the large imposing Griffin Tazza, central to the whole gardens. The centre of the Broad Walk was previously occupied by the Swan fountain (1874–1960), then by the Boy and Dolphin (1962–94), the latter now returned to Hyde Park.

The Avenue Gardens. © Peter Jeffree

Tazza means large 'vase'. The one remaining original is constructed in composition stone. In 1828 Felix Austin started making artificial stone. His works were in New Road, Fitzroy Square, more or less opposite Holy Trinity Church. He also had premises with John Seeley at 24 Church Street, Rotherhithe. From 1840 he partnered with Seeley to produce artificial garden ornaments.

The mix is Portland cement, broken stone, pounded marble and coarse sand. The moulds were bought from a Mr Powell who had tried to rival Eleanor Coade with a manufactory at Bow, but he went out of business. The 1841 first catalogue states, 'the stone is of a light tint, requires no painting or colouring, will not sustain injury from the severest winter, and being impervious to wet, is particularly applicable to all kinds of water works. Its superiority is now so thoroughly established that the most eminent architects and scientific gentlemen have expressed, in their highest terms, their approbation of its durability, and close resemblance to the real stone.' Supported by Queen Victoria, the firm continued until at least 1872.

The Readymoney Fountain

At the north end of the Broad Walk is the rather weathered Gothic Readymoney fountain, erected in 1869 and made from Sicilian marble and polished red Aberdeen granite. It was the gift of Sir Cowasjee Jehangir, a wealthy Parsee from Bombay who wished to thank the English people for the protection given to the Parsees under British rule in India. Readymoney was a nickname given to the family, who adopted it as a surname. Sir Cowasjee was made a Companion of the Star of India in recognition of his many donations to charity and he was known as 'The Peabody of the East' as well as 'The Peabody of Bombay'.

On the fountain are reliefs of Queen Victoria and Prince Albert, and the donor as well as a lion and Brahmin bull. All the great and the good were there for the unveiling in the presence of the Prince and Princess of Teck (parents of Queen Mary, wife of King George V), and the Nawab of Bengal.

This is one of the many fountains commissioned by the Metropolitan Drinking Fountain Association which was founded in 1859 by Samuel Gurney to provide much needed fresh water for visitors in parks around the country. Robert Kierle was its architect. The first fountain was opened on 21 April 1859 at Snow Hill in the City of London. By 1878 there were more than 700 fountains. Fresh drinking water was a huge issue, particularly in London, where cholera had taken its toll. Every year the association would report on its financial position, listing the donors. It is interesting to note that £100 was donated yearly by the monarch and £105 by the

The Readymoney Fountain. © Peter Jeffree

City of London. Today the Drinking Fountain Association still exists and its objectives are very similar: 'To promote the provision of drinking water to people and animals in the United Kingdom and overseas, and the preservation of the Association's archive materials, artefacts, drinking fountains, cattle troughs and other installations.'

Regent's Park Gates

Queen Mary's gardens are entered by the black and gold Jubilee Gates, the gardens on the site of the former Royal Botanical Society's gardens. The gates were donated by Sigismund Goetze, as were those at Chester Gate. Goetze was a wealthy and successful artist who from 1909 to 1939 lived in Grove House (now Nuffield House) on the northern perimeter of the park. The Jubilee Gates commemorate the silver jubilee and official opening of Queen Mary's gardens in 1935.

Open Air Theatre

With one of the largest auditoria in London, Regent's Park Open Air Theatre is the oldest professional, permanent outdoor, theatre in Britain and their annual 18-week season is attended by over 140,000 each year. In 1932, the early closure of a disastrous play by Italian dictator, Benito Mussolini, left the New Theatre – now the Noël

Chester Gate. © Peter Jeffree

Coward – in desperate need of a production. Robert Atkins and Sydney Carroll presented a 'black and white' production of *Twelfth Night,* which they subsequently transferred to a makeshift theatre in Regent's Park.

A year later, the first full season included a revival of the previous year's *Twelfth Night* and the first of almost fifty different productions of *A Midsummer Night's Dream* to play at the theatre over the next 80 years. By 1939, the country was at war and the theatre produced matinee-only seasons due to the blackouts. Regent's Park Open Air Theatre and the Windmill Theatre were the only two theatres in London to remain open throughout the war. Between 1945 and 1955, post-war

comedies dominated the programme but were balanced with *King John* (1948), *Faust* (1949), *The Winter's Tale* (1950) and *Cymbeline* (1952).

In 1953, brick dressing rooms were built behind the stage, replacing the tents that had been used previously. By 1962, the company were invited to perform *Twelfth Night* and *Hamlet* at the *Baalbek Festival* in Lebanon. This marked the first of many Open Air Theatre overseas engagements; over the following years, in conjunction with the British Council, the company performed in over twenty different countries including Dubai, Russia, Israel and Egypt.

In 1974, major changes occurred. The current, fixed amphitheatre-style, auditorium was built at a cost

The entrance to the open air theatre. © Peter Jeffree

of £150,000 followed by a workshop, a new box office, kitchen and picnic lawn. Delays in the building project caused the following season, which included *The Taming of the Shrew* with Jeremy Irons and Zoë Wannamaker, to be staged at the Roundhouse. This saw the theatre and their many productions through to the Millennium.

However, by 2000, at a cost of two million pounds, major building work commenced to refurbish the auditorium and public areas of the theatre and to build the Robert Atkins Studio. 2010 saw further improvements as fundraising began for a building project that included a new box office, dressing room complex and office suite built on site, in time for the 2012 season. By 2018 at a cost of £2.8m, new kitchens and the Regent's Park Rehearsal Studios were opened.

A hidden gem at Regent's Park – St John's Lodge Garden

St John's Lodge Garden, located to the north of the Inner Circle, was designed as a series of compartments ornamented with sculpture and stonework. It was made to be a garden 'fit for meditation' by Robert Weir Schultz in 1889. The centrepiece to the garden was originally St John the Baptist, but this has been replaced by Hylas and the Nymph statue by Henry Pegram.

Also, located within the garden is the Goatherd's Daughter statue. This Grade II listed bronze statue of a woman carrying a young goat was erected in honour of Harold and Gertrude Baillie Weaver by the National Council for Animal Welfare in 1932. Designed by Charles Leonard Harwell, he received the Royal British Society of Sculptors Silver Medal for this statue. The inscription reads: 'To all the Protectors of the Defenceless'. While St John's Lodge itself is a private residence, visitors can still access the garden through a small gate along the Inner Circle, near the park office.

St John's Lodge was originally built in 1818 by John Raffield. It was the second villa in the park to be occupied. In 1847 it belonged to the wealthy and eminent Goldsmid brothers and was greatly enlarged by Charles Barry. In 1889 the lease was acquired by the 3rd Marquess of Bute, who commissioned Robert Weir Schultz to improve the garden layout. The building was later used as a hospital for disabled officers during the First World War. It was the Headquarters of St Dunstan's from 1921–1937 and the Institute of Archaeology 1937–58. It is now a private residence, with public access to the garden. A monument of boys with armorial shields on pillars stands in the garden in front of the lodge. Likely installed for the Marquess of Bute, three were designed by Sir William Goscombe John in 1894, one by Harold Youngman in 1938 and the remaining two are undated.

St John's Lodge Garden.

John Nash (1752–1835)

The architect John Nash designed a significant portion of Regency London, leaving a legacy to rival that of Sir Christopher Wren. His most famous works are Regent Street, Regent's Park and, outside London, the Brighton Pavilion.

Nash is commemorated today with a blue plaque at 66 Bloomsbury Square, the end unit of a six-house terrace which he designed himself. Located on Great Russell Street, the terrace is his earliest known project to survive and was one of the first developments to be clad in stucco – a feature that later became a standard part of the London streetscape.

Nash's time at Bloomsbury Square was overshadowed by emotional and financial turmoil. He moved there not long after separating from his wife, Jane, in June 1778. Although they reunited at number 66 for several months in 1779, Nash started divorce proceedings the following year. Among his complaints were that his wife had simulated pregnancies, imposed two children on him who were not his own and had run up bills of nearly £300 on hats. The Bloomsbury project failed financially and Nash was declared bankrupt in 1783.

Nash returned to London in 1797 following a period of exile in Wales, during which he rebuilt his career and established himself as the leading exponent of the picturesque. He was able to apply his picturesque principles to an urban landscape on a grand scale when in 1811 he was commissioned to develop the Crown Estate of Marylebone Park. The result, 15 years later, was Regent Street, Regent's Park, the surrounding stuccoed Palladian terraces, and Park Village. Nash was also a leading promoter of the Regent's Canal, the first section of which opened in 1816. Later, his improvements to London's West End, completed in 1831, set the footprint for Trafalgar Square.

In 1815, on a personal commission from the Prince Regent, Nash started work on what became his best-known building, the Royal Pavilion at Brighton. Over eight years he transformed this former farmhouse into a Mughal-inspired fantasy of onion domes and minarets and built a new banqueting room, a corridor gallery and a suite of royal apartments. Extravagant inside and out, it defined the stylistic excesses of the Regency era.

His reconstruction work on Buckingham Palace wasn't as successful. Nash was employed at the insistence of King George IV (the former Prince Regent), but the ambitious remodelling project was planned and executed in haste. Some of Nash's new, single-storey wings had to be rebuilt, and he let the

Thomas Lawrence, Portrait of John Nash (1827) at the age of seventy-two. Courtesy of the Principal, Fellow and Scholars of Jesus College, Oxford

budget spiral to more than two and half times the original estimate. On the king's death in 1830, Nash's fortunes also declined and he died five years later on 13 May 1835, with Buckingham Palace still incomplete.

William Andrews Nesfield (1794–1881)

William Andrews Nesfield was born in Chester-le-Street and was the son of the rector of Brancepath, Durham. He was educated at Winchester, Trinity College, Cambridge and Woolwich. Nesfield joined the army in 1809 and served in the Peninsular war under the command of the Duke of Wellington. He retired from the army in 1816, embarking on a career in painting, being influenced by the work of Turner and G.F. Robson. He was a member of the Old Water Colour Society from 1823 until 1851. Nesfield, although a competent water colourist, found his true vocation in landscape design. He gained his first commission in 1836, which heralded the start of a long and flourishing career. He worked on over 260 estates belonging to the rich and influential people of the day.

In 1844, Nesfield was asked to redesign the arboretum at Kew Gardens, which had become overcrowded. His plans were extensive and included several vistas radiating from the palm house, a parterre, the remodelling of the formal landscape around the palm house as well as the palm house pond. One vista faced south and was called the pagoda vista, another facing west toward the Thames was named the Syon vista. The structure of Nesfield's formal landscape still largely survives today.

In 1860 Nesfield designed the gardens of the Royal Horticultural Society where his formal designs were fully realised. Nesfield's many commissions included work on many London parks including here in Regent's Park. He drew inspiration from pre-eighteenth century English Garden styles and was particularly good at designing terraces and parterres. He designed the terrace garden at Holkham Hall in 1854. Nesfield's work can be admired also at Rode Hall, Witley Court, Worsley Hall, Grimston Park, Broughton Hall, Ogston Hall, Doddington Place Gardens, Wroxton Abbey and Castle Howard.

9

KENSINGTON GARDENS

A ROYAL PARK WITH A ROYAL PALACE

It would seem that our veteran correspondent Richard Church was somewhat fond of Kensington Gardens, becoming almost poetic in some of his descriptions here: 'The view from the east front of the Palace, right through Kensington toward London, is majestic. It remains as a monument to a way of life that has vanished along with the sedan chair, the harpsichord and the three-cornered hat. The great trees, standing like galleons, so that one half expects them to move together, as a fleet, over the lawns, are so disposed about the landscape that glimpses are offered, here and there, of further and further reaches of parkland, fading into the London air, whose half tangible fumes reduce the brightness of the green, so that it becomes almost unreal, a canvas by an old master of landscape painting, a John Crome or a Peter de Wint, its quality more than "half as old as time".'

Today, the 275 acres of Kensington Gardens have a genteel charm and they are quieter than many of the other Royal Parks with little impact from nearby traffic. The nearest to traffic generated comes from prams, pushchairs and roller-skaters. This is a Royal Park that is popular with children; with open stretches for flying kites, to the model sailing boats on the round pond, the playground and of course Peter Pan himself.

When the asthmatic Dutch king, William III, came to England he rejected the damp Greenwich Palace in favour of Kensington House, which he bought in 1689 for 18,000 guineas. Sir Christopher Wren refurbished the building with William and Mary, both ardent gardeners, taking on the task of the redeveloping of 26 acres of the palace gardens. They promoted the Dutch style in gardens which included enclosed areas with neat flowerbeds

A Front View of the Royal Palace of Kensington, 1751. © Yale Center for British Art, Paul Mellon Collection

and well-trimmed yew, holly and box hedges, eventually swept away when Anne, Mary's sister, became queen. She preferred an English garden and added a further 30 acres, adding a ha-ha as well as creating a sunken garden on the site of a gravel-pit. In 1702, Sir John Vanbrugh and Nicholas Hawksmoor designed an orangery where she could hold soirées. Kensington Gardens today owes its present style to the wife of George II. It was Queen Caroline who separated them from Hyde Park with the assistance of royal gardener Charles Bridgeman. Great avenues of trees were planted, and in particular the 50-feet-wide Broad Walk, running up from the palace gate towards Black Lion Gate in the north. The round pond was another addition, designed to be seen from the palace windows, a classical temple, and the Long Water, a continuation of the Serpentine. During George II's reign, Kensington Gardens were open to visitors at weekends whilst the king was absent, but formal dress was compulsory. George III was rarely at Kensington and the royal apartments were closed for 40 years, with the public now having greater access from the nineteenth century.

In 1837 Kensington Gardens further lost its spot in the limelight when Queen Victoria, despite being born at

Kensington Palace, moved the court to Buckingham Palace. It was felt that the gardens did not need updating and only a few changes were made during the nineteenth and twentieth centuries. Most of the ha-ha was filled in and West Carriage Drive became the new boundary of Kensington Gardens and Hyde Park. The ornamental Italian Gardens were added in 1860 and in 1909 a new sunken garden was made outside Kensington Palace.

The gardens also became a significant place of remembrance and none more spectacular than the addition of the Albert Memorial for Queen Victoria's husband situated on the edge of the gardens. There are statues of John Hanning Speke, the explorer who discovered the source of the Nile, Edward Jenner, who developed a vaccine for smallpox, and even Peter Pan. In 2000, a children's playground opened in memory of the late Diana, Princess of Wales.

NOT TO BE MISSED ON A VISIT TO KENSINGTON GARDENS

Kensington Palace

Kensington Palace lies at the top of the Broad Walk. It is surprisingly modest in scale for a royal residence, particularly from the age of Louis XIV. It only consists of two façades, with the remainder comprising buildings gathered around three courtyards. The south frontage, which was built in 1689–95 for William III, contains the King's Gallery and was possibly designed by Sir Christopher

Kensington Palace. © Peter Jeffree

Wren. However, its more restrained style is close to contemporary Dutch architecture. The east front was rebuilt in 1718–26 for George I and is centred on a fine Venetian window which reflects the new Palladian style.

The Orangery

While original orangeries herald from Renaissance Italy, these structures first appeared on British soil as a place for wealthy landowners to keep delicate citrus trees to protect them from our harsh winter frosts. At the time glass was an expensive commodity, and therefore the orangery soon found fashion amongst the higher classes as a symbol of

grandeur and extravagance. As imported fruit such as pineapples became more widely available, some households would place a stove within their orangeries to provide additional heat.

With developments such as the abolition of the window tax and advancements in glass-making technology, the nineteenth century saw glazed roofs introduced to orangery designs in order to allow as much sunlight into the building as possible, which also increased their decadence and desirability.

Built between 1704–5, the iconic orangery at Kensington Palace was designed by Nicholas Hawksmoor, an architect famed for his representation

The Orangery Restaurant. © Peter Jeffree

of the English Baroque style, popular across Europe in the seventeenth century for its decorative appearance. The orangery was originally built for Queen Anne, partly for housing fruit but also as a lavish entertainment venue for her party guests. The palace orangery pre-dates the introduction of glazed roofs, and so gets the majority of its natural light source from the rows of towering, white-framed windows that run the length of the building – each one consisting of thirty six square glass panels. It was later altered by Vanbrugh.

The Serpentine Gallery

The Serpentine Gallery was built as a refreshment room in 1934 by Henry Tanner Jr to replace an earlier refreshment pavilion. It now displays a wide range of art exhibitions and contemporary art both internally as well as externally. It was established by the Arts Council of Great Britain in 1970. Notable artists who have been exhibited here include Man Ray, Henry Moore, Jean-Michel Basquiat, Andy Warhol, Paula Rego, Bridget Riley, Allan McCollum, Anish Kapoor, Christian Boltanski, Philippe Parreno, Richard Prince, Wolfgang Tillmans, Gerhard Richter, Gustav Metzger, Damien Hirst and Jeff Koons.

Serpentine Sackler Gallery

Across the bridge separating Hyde Park from Kensington Gardens is the former Powder Magazine, used originally as a building for storing gunpowder. It is now the Serpentine

The Serpentine Gallery. © Ben Abel

The Serpentine Sackler Gallery.

Sackler Gallery. It was built in 1805 and remodelled in the 1820s, probably by Decimus Burton, and later became a tea room.

The Italian Gardens

At the far end of the Long Water are the Italian Gardens, which were constructed in 1860–61 when the Westbourne river was cut off and a new well sunk to supply the park with water. Their formal and architectural style contrasts sharply with the pastoral setting of the wider park. Behind the Italianate loggia, which doubles as a pumphouse, are the arched remains of a former head wall outlet. Designed by Banks and Barry, the marble fountain and balustrading were by John Thomas. The gardens were initially promoted by Prince Albert.

The Italian Gardens. © Peter Jeffree

Cascades in the Italian Gardens. © Peter Jeffree

Edward Jenner

The bronze statue of Edward Jenner commemorates the surgeon who introduced vaccination against the smallpox that killed thousands of people in eighteenth-century England. He realised that people who handled cows rarely got smallpox and used cowpox as a vaccine against the disease. His statue, by William Calder Marshall, was erected in Trafalgar Square in 1858, but the authorities soon felt that the setting, among naval and military heroes, was inappropriate and suggested moving it. After much deliberation, he was moved to Kensington Gardens in 1862.

Edward Jenner.

Peter Pan

One of the most popular statues in London is Peter Pan, overlooking the Long Water. It is also the best-known work of Sir George Frampton. Peter was the creation of J.M. Barrie, who lived on Bayswater Road. The Darling family in his stories was inspired by the Llewellyn Davies family, whom he met in Kensington Gardens. In 1906 Barrie decided to create a statue of Peter Pan and took photographs of the young Michael Llewellyn Davies in costume, and commissioned Sir George Frampton to make it. In 1912, the statue was put up over two days behind curtains, which were removed overnight so that it seemed to have appeared as if by magic. Barrie put an announcement in *The Times* informing its readers that there was 'a surprise in store for the children who go to Kensington Gardens to feed the ducks in the Serpentine this morning.' There were complaints in parliament about the author promoting his work in a public park, but it soon became an overwhelming success with copies elsewhere, in particular Liverpool's Sefton Park. The statue shows Peter playing his pipes on a tree stump surrounded by rabbits, mice, squirrels and fairies.

Peter Pan. © Peter Jeffree

The Albert Memorial

The most lavish of all London's monuments is also found in Kensington Gardens and is the stunning Albert Memorial, which stands opposite the Royal Albert Hall, close to the site of the Great Exhibition of 1851. It commemorates the life and work of Prince Albert. A month after his death, plans were put in place to find a way to commemorate him with a fitting monument through public subscription. Seven architects were invited to offer designs for a memorial, but the one chosen by the queen was the Gothic scheme of George Gilbert Scott, which was based on medieval shrines, including the Eleanor Crosses. It is a complex memorial and based on Albert's interests and passions and, in particular, on the themes of the Great Exhibition, of which he was the prime mover.

At the outer corners are sculptural groups of the continents of Europe, Asia, Africa and America, representing the nations which exhibited at the Great Exhibition, and the groups above the frieze are symbolic of agriculture, manufacture, commerce and engineering, the major themes of the exhibition. The Parnassus frieze, which runs around the memorial, depicts those persons the Victorians considered to be the greatest figures in western culture, arranged by the subjects of poetry, music, painting, sculpture and architecture.

The Albert Memorial. © Peter Jeffree

Work began in September 1864 and it took eight years to complete. The figure of Albert proved to be more challenging, with the sculptor Baron Marochetti chosen by Victoria. Both his designs were unsatisfactory and he died in 1867. The commission was then given to John Foley who finished the giant statue in 1873, but he too died before it was even cast. It was Thomas Brock who completed the work. The gilded figure shows Albert seated in Garter robes, and holding a volume of the Great Exhibition catalogue. The memorial was opened to the public in 1872, with the statue installed in 1875 and unveiled in March 1876. Scott was knighted for his work on the Albert Memorial. Despite damage during the Second World War, it has survived remarkably well and was eventually subject to an £11.2 million restoration during the 1990s. In October 1998, Queen Elizabeth II unveiled the newly resplendent restored monument to her great-great-grandfather and it is still considered the finest of Victorian monuments in London and beyond.

A hidden gem at Kensington Gardens

In an interview given by Henry Moore in 1980, he said that: 'After the 1978 exhibition at the Serpentine Gallery in London, in which several large pieces were located in Kensington Gardens, there was a request for me to leave a sculpture there permanently, which I agreed to do. I thought the Large Arch was very naturally sited, particularly as it could be seen reflected in the water from across the lake.' During the

Henry Moore's arch. © Peter Jeffree

exhibition, many people believed the sculpture to be made of marble, but in fact it was a fibre-glass exhibition cast made originally for his exhibition at the Forte di Belvedere in Florence (1963), because of the difficulty of getting a very heavy bronze or marble on to the site. Therefore, so that it could be left as a permanent sculpture in Kensington Gardens, Moore produced a version in travertine marble which is a very lasting material. The Arch was found to be unstable in 1996 and was subsequently dismantled and placed into storage. It was restored and replaced in its original location in 2012.

INVOLVED WITH KENSINGTON GARDENS

George Gilbert Scott (1811–1878)

Sir George Gilbert Scott was the founder of a successful architectural dynasty, and possibly the most successful and prolific Victorian Gothic architect. His output was incredible, and he worked in almost every part of the country.

Scott was born in Gawcott, Buckinghamshire, the son of a poor clergyman. He studied architecture with James Esmeston, then worked in the offices of Henry Roberts and then with Sampson Kempthorne. He was not well off, so Scott had trouble launching his own practice. As a result, he found work where he could – much of it designing workhouses and gaols. His best known early design was Reading Gaol. He eventually travelled to France, studying Gothic cathedrals and parochial churches. It was these studies that helped form his own vision of architecture, which was heavily influenced by French High Gothic (1280–1340). Scott believed passionately in the Gothic Revival; his view was that the Gothic style was the only suitable style for both secular and ecclesiastical buildings.

His most important early church design was St Giles, Camberwell, London (1841–4). St Giles established Scott's name as a Gothic Revival architect. Many commissions followed, including town churches like St George's, Doncaster, and St Matthias, Richmond. Along with these new designs came a huge quantity of work restoring older churches, often sweeping away original work and replacing it with his own meticulously crafted 'improved' Gothic. He was hired to oversee restoration work on many of England's cathedrals and became Surveyor of the fabric for Westminster Abbey.

It is not for a church that Scott's name is best remembered, however, but for a London landmark. When Prince Albert, Queen Victoria's beloved consort, died in 1861 it was decided to erect a memorial to him in Kensington Gardens. A design competition was held, and

George Gilbert Scott.

Sir George Frampton (1860–1928)

Sir George James Frampton was a British sculptor. He was a leading member of the New Sculpture movement in his early career when he created sculptures with elements of Art Nouveau and Symbolism, often combining various materials such as marble and bronze in a single piece. While his later works were more traditional in style, Frampton had a prolific career in which he created many notable public monuments, including several statues of Queen Victoria and later, after the First World War, a number of war memorials. These included the Edith Cavell Memorial in London, which, along with the Peter Pan statue here in Kensington Gardens, are possibly Frampton's best known works.

Scott's exquisitely gilded design won. It would be hard to find a more striking example of Victorian Gothic style. Scott's design was a mix of Byzantine and medieval design, with the brooding sculpture of the prince beneath an ornate canopy decorated with marble, precious metals, and enamel.

Scott's most prominent civic commission was the Foreign and War Offices in Whitehall (now the Foreign and Commonwealth Offices). Here he ran headlong into a stubborn Lord Palmerston, who insisted on a neo-classical design. The argument provoked a public reaction which might seem puzzling to modern eyes, but at the time it was a real clash of values. In the end, Palmerston was victorious, and Scott designed the buildings in the style of an Italian Renaissance palace. Scott died in 1878 and is buried in Westminster Abbey.

George James Frampton (1860–1928) by W.H. Latham.

10

THE WILDLIFE OF THE ROYAL PARKS

The Royal Parks are teeming with wildlife, from jackdaws resting and hiding in the tree canopies, to deer resting under ancient and veteran oaks, along with pelicans perching on park benches. You may hear tawny owls calling at dusk and find tiny voles nesting in the grass meadows. We are surrounded by flora and fauna and the numbers are incredible.

The millions of visitors can experience wildlife in its natural setting and this is what makes the Royal Parks so special. The 5,000 acres that the Royal Parks charity manage have an incredibly diverse range of habitats,

Richmond Park – wildlife up close and personal. © Peter Jeffree

which support a rich variety of wildlife. These parks are home and haven to some of our rarest or protected species, from stag beetles to bats, great crested newts, and grass snakes.

The history of these parks is huge and wildlife within them is woven into their histories. For instance, the herds of red and fallow deer which still roam free in Richmond Park and Bushy Park date back hundreds of years. Much of this wildlife is visible to many of us but an even greater variety of species are often almost invisible. This may include timid goldcrests hiding in the hedgerows, purple emperor butterflies in Richmond Park, or the thousands of invertebrate species and mini beasts at ground level, and below.

It's often the birdlife that is most noticeable on a visit to many of the parks. There are over 200 species in Regent's Park alone including sparrowhawks to owls, thrushes and all three native species of woodpeckers. Waterfowl and wetlands are home to thousands of waterfowl and wading birds, including grey heron and rare kingfishers, with the parks having over forty ponds and lakes, wetlands and reedbeds.

There are over 170,000 trees in the Royal Parks, and these woodlands and trees are major habitats for birds. Grasslands dominate many of the parks and these are rich food sources for native birds such as starlings, green woodpecker and mistle thrush, and the

A heron in Bushy Park. © Dave Rotherham

Veteran trees in Richmond Park.

Deer in Bushy Park – a common sight here and in Richmond Park.

nationally rare skylark, which nests in the wide-open grasslands of Richmond and Bushy Parks. Even dead and where dead and decaying wood is left, these provide a wonderfully rich micro habitat for insects and beetles.

The red and fallow deer roaming Richmond and Bushy Parks are some of the best-known animals and have been grazing the parks since the 1600s when the parks were enclosed as royal hunting grounds. Historically they've played a key role in shaping the landscape by browsing the trees, and even now, they help maintain the acid grassland habitat by grazing.

Bats are often sighted at dusk in many of the parks, and can include the common pipistrelle, soprano pipistrelle, noctule and Leisler's Bat. They can be seen flitting above the lakes in St James's Park and Regent's Park, hunting for insects.

Among the many grasslands can be found many smaller mammals. The parks are home to bank voles and field mice, who play a key role in dispersing seeds and are a food source for bigger animals and birds of prey, including owls.

Invertebrates are animals without a backbone such as insects, spiders, snails and earthworms. They pollinate flowers, control pests, create soil and recycle organic matter and they're also a major food source for birds,

The city is never far away, viewed here from Richmond Park. © Peter Jeffree

and other wildlife. Without them, food chains and food webs would fall apart. Life on earth depends on invertebrates. They make up over 95% of animals worldwide. In the Royal Parks, all the other wildlife relies on invertebrates for survival. They may be some of our smallest animals – but they're most critical to the long-term health of the parks, and their biodiversity. There are over 4,700 species that live within them. These tiny creatures are so fundamental to the future of both the Royal Parks and the planet.

Amphibians are extremely sensitive to changes in temperature or low rainfall, which makes them particularly vulnerable to climate change. Great care is taken to ensure the park ponds, lakes and streams are kept as clean as possible, and water levels managed. Monitoring and surveying amphibian populations can give early warnings of climate-related changes in the parks. Frogs like to stay close to their breeding ponds, even when they aren't breeding, and can hibernate in pond mud or under log piles. Toads often live further away from water and migrate back and forth during breeding and hibernation. Some of the shyest wildlife in the Royal Parks are snakes and lizards but they can occasionally be seen basking in the sunshine on a path or rock. Biodiversity, with our ever-changing climate, has never been more important and the Royal Parks have a vital role to play in our capital city.

AND FINALLY...

The final word rests with our old friend Richard Church. He concludes in his 1956 guide that 'these Royal Parks are a facet of our democratic community, an expression of something possessed in pride and maintained in mutuality. They show our English tradition as a living body, flowering here and now, with roots set firmly in our past.' Nearly 70 years later, his words are as relevant today as they were decades before.

FURTHER READING

Books

Ashton, John. *Hyde Park – from Domesday Book to Date*, Downey and Co. London, 1896.

Baxter Brown, Michael. *Richmond Park – The History of a Royal Deer Park*, Robert Hale, London, 1985.

Braybrooke, Neville. *London Green, the story of Kensington Gardens, Hyde Park, Green Park & St James's Park*, Victor Gollancz Ltd, London, 1959.

Cecil, Lady Evelyn. *London Parks and Gardens*, Archibald Constable, London, 1907.

Church, Richard. *London's Royal Parks – An Appreciation by Richard Church*, HMSO, London, 1956.

Collenette, C.L. *A History of Richmond Park*, S.R. Publishers Limited, Wakefield, 1971.

Conville, David. *The Park – The Story of the Open Air Theatre, Regent's Park*, Oberon Books, London, 2007.

Dancy, Eric. *Hyde Park*, Methuen & Co. Ltd, London, 1937.

Edgar, Donald. *The Royal Parks*, W.H. Allen, London, 1986.

Friends of Richmond Park. *Guide to Richmond Park*, Richmond, 2011.

Jones, Pamela Fletcher. *Richmond Park – Portrait of a Royal Playground*, Phillimore, Chichester, 1972.

Jones, Andrew. *The Buildings of Green Park – A tour of certain buildings, monuments and other structures in Mayfair and St James's*, ACC Art Books, Woodbridge, 2020.

Lankester, Max. *What's in a name? Features of Richmond Park*, The Friends of Richmond Park, 2015.

Larwood, Jacob. *The Story of The London Parks*, Chatto and Windus, London, 1900.

McDowall, David. *Richmond Park – The Walker's Historical Guide*, Richmond, 1996.

Quiney, Anthony. *A Year in the Life of Greenwich Park*, Frances Lincoln Ltd, London, 2009.

Rabbitts, Paul. *Richmond Park: From Medieval Pasture to Royal Park*, Amberley Publishing, Stroud, 2016.

Rabbitts, Paul. *Sir Christopher Wren*, Shire Publications, Oxford, 2019.

Rabbitts, Paul. *London's Royal Parks*, Shire Publications, Oxford, 2014.

Rabbitts, Paul. *Hyde Park: The People's Park*, Amberley Publishing, Stroud, 2015.

Rabbitts, Paul. *Regent's Park: From Tudor Hunting Ground to the Present*, Amberley Publishing, Stroud, 2014.

Royal Parks. *London's Royal Parks Souvenir Guide*, The Royal Parks, London, 1993.

Royal Parks. *Guide to The Regent's Park and Primrose Hill*, Essential Books Ltd, London, 1999.

Royal Parks. *Buildings and Monuments in the Royal Parks*, The Royal Parks, London, 1997.

Royal Parks Foundation. *London's Royal Parks*, Think Publishing, London, 2006.

Saunders, Ann. *Regent's Park – A Study of the Development of the Area from 1086 to the Present Day*, David & Charles, Newton Abbot, 1969.

Sheppard, Martin. *Regent's Park and Primrose Hill*, Frances Lincoln Ltd, London, 2010.

Tweedie, Mrs Alec. *Hyde Park, its history and romance*, Besant & Co. Ltd, London, 1930.

Webster, A.D. *Greenwich Park – Its History and Associations*, Conway Maritime Press, London, 1902.

Webster, A.D. *The Regent's Park and Primrose Hill*, Greening & Co. Ltd, London, 1911.

White, Kathy; Foster, Peter. *Bushy Park – Royals, Rangers and Rogues*, Foundry Press, East Molesey, 1997.

Williams, Guy. *The Royal Parks of London*, Constable, London, 1978.

Acknowledgements

My thanks to all those who contributed to the many photographs throughout the book, and in particular Peter Jeffree who takes great joy in capturing the many parks he visits and, most of all, London's Royal Parks. As ever, my sincere gratitude to my wife Julie and daughter Ellie, for unwavering support in all my writings and ramblings and forays into the country's public parks and London's Royal Parks.